Betty Crocker

D0795554

Bisquick® to the Rescue

WILEY

Wiley Publishing, Inc.

Copyright © 2011 by General Mills, Minneapolis, Minnesota. All rights reserved.

Published by Wiley Publishing, Inc., Hoboken, New Jersey

Published simultaneously in Canada

For general information on our other products and services or for technical support, please contact our Customer Care Department within the United States at (877) 762-2974, outside the United States at (317) 572-3993 or fax (317) 572-4002.

Wiley also publishes its books in a variety of electronic formats. Some content that appears in print may not be available in electronic books. For more information about Wiley products, visit our web site at www.wiley.com.

Library of Congress Cataloging-in-Publication Data:

Betty Crocker Bisquick to the rescue.
       p. cm.
  Includes index.
  ISBN 978-0-470-91657-5 (pbk.); ISBN 978-0-470-94687-9 (ebk); ISBN 978-0-470-94686-2 (ebk); ISBN 978-0-470-94688-6 (ebk).
  1. Cooking, American. 2. Quick and easy cooking. I. Crocker, Betty. II. Title: Bisquick to the rescue.
  TX715.B488825 2011
  641.5973--dc22

                                  2010040945

Manufactured in the United States of America

10 9 8 7 6 5 4 3 2 1

Cover photos: Spiced Tilapia with Honeyed Mango-Lime Sauce (page 170), Easy Chicken Pot Pie (page 130), Gluten Free Pancakes (page 19), Beer-Battered Fish (page 177)

GENERAL MILLS

Editorial Director: *Jeff Nowak*

Publishing Manager: *Christine Gray*

Editors: *Grace Wells, Karen Schiemo, Kathy Saatzer*

Recipe Development and Testing: *Betty Crocker Kitchens*

Photography: *General Mills Photography Studios and Image Library*

Photographer: *Chuck Nields*

Food Stylists: *Nancy Johnson, Amy Peterson*

WILEY PUBLISHING, INC.

Publisher: *Natalie Chapman*

Associate Publisher: *Jessica Goodman*

Executive Editor: *Anne Ficklen*

Editor: *Charleen Barila*

Production Editor: *Liz Britten*

Cover Design: *Jeffrey Faust*

Interior Design and Layout: *Indianapolis Composition Services*

Manufacturing Manager: *Kevin Watt*

The Betty Crocker Kitchens seal guarantees success in your kitchen. Every recipe has been tested in America's Most Trusted Kitchens™ to meet our high standards of reliability, easy preparation and great taste.

Find more great ideas at *BettyCrocker*.com

Dear Friends,

Who hasn't had one of those days? You're late getting home from work . . . one child is waiting to be picked up from piano lessons . . . another is scrambling to finish homework before heading to practice . . . the family is famished. And you're in panic mode pondering how to get a wholesome, satisfying meal on the table with no time to spare.

We heard the distress calls from harried cooks across the country and created this lifeline for round-the-clock dining dilemmas. It's *Bisquick® to the Rescue*! All 104 recipes depend on tried-and-true Bisquick to produce delicious dishes that have outstanding, homemade flavor without the from-scratch fuss.

You don't need a superhero—just a box of Bisquick—to make such rise-and-shine selections as Apples 'n Brown Sugar Coffee Cake (page 118) and Vegetable-Cheese Strata (page 48). When midday munchies attack, reach for Mini Chinese Chicken Snacks (page 63), and Sesame Pork Strips (page 64). Bisquick also beats the clock at dinnertime by giving a head start to Macaroni and Cheese Pie (page 156), Beer-Battered Fish (page 177) and Salsa Burrito Bake (page 141). Dessert during the week? Miracles can be done when Citrus Mini Cheesecakes (page 192) and Triple-Chocolate Bars (page 228) are on the menu!

And be sure to check out the winners of the Better with Bisquick Recipe Contest, including our top three finishers: Double-Chocolate Strawberry Pancakes (page 25), Spiced Tilapia with Honeyed Mango-Lime Sauce (page 171) and Buffalo Chicken Pie (page 125).

Bisquick to the Rescue includes mealtime solutions for everyone, including those on restricted diets by offering gluten-free versions of comforting classics like Chicken and Dumplings, Cinnamon Streusel Coffee Cake, Cheese Garlic Biscuits and Strawberry Shortcakes!

Fast, fresh and flavorful, Bisquick rescues you from mealtime misery. So grab a box and head to the kitchen with confidence!

Grace Wells

Grace Wells

Contents

Bisquick Contest Winners Make Mealtime a Breeze!

Between driving home from work and shuttling the kids to their events, most cooks are time-pressed during the dinner hour. You want to provide loved ones a supper that's both wholesome and hearty. But how do you offer from-scratch flavor with little fuss? The winners of our Better with Bisquick Recipe Contest deliciously prove that Bisquick is the key to preparing family-friendly foods that are fast, fresh and fabulous!

Grand-prize winner Joni Hilton takes plain pancakes to a whole new level by combining Bisquick with sour cream and two kinds of chocolate. She then tops the flapjacks with whipped cream, sliced fruit and strawberry syrup to create Double-Chocolate Strawberry Pancakes (page 25). These incredible hotcakes will wake up tired taste buds at breakfast—but they're so indulgent, you could also serve them for dessert.

For a main course that your family will fall for hook, line and sinker, try Veronica Callaghan's Spiced Tilapia with Honeyed Mango-Lime Sauce (page 171). Bisquick lends a crunchy coating to the fish in this super second-place recipe.

Buffalo Chicken Pie (page 125), a third-place finisher from Jamie Jones, captures the zesty taste of hot wings and is topped with a golden brown Bisquick crust.

You'll find these winning recipes—and 13 wonderful runners-up—throughout this book. Each and every one is family pleasing, fresh tasting and features tried-and-true Bisquick! Here are the top 3 recipes, the amount they won and a description of the recipe in their own words.

BETTER WITH BISQUICK

Grand Prize Winner—$1,000

Contestant Name: Joni Hilton

Recipe Name: Double-Chocolate Strawberry Pancakes (page 25)

Description: "This is a true flavor blast of chocolate and strawberry—double doses of each! Everyone loves chocolate-dipped strawberries, so I thought a pancake combining those yummy flavors would be a real hit."

2nd Place Winner—$500

Contestant Name: Veronica Callaghan

Recipe Name: Spiced Tilapia with Honeyed Mango-Lime Sauce (page 171)

Description: "This spicy-sweet fish dish has dining-out elegance with dining-in ease. The crisp tilapia fillets are cooled by a tangy mango sauce."

3rd Place Winner—$250

Contestant Name: Jamie Jones

Recipe Name: Buffalo Chicken Pie (page 124)

Description: "This recipe came about the Monday after the Super Bowl, when I needed a quick and easy dish for dinner for my busy family. I opened the fridge and had leftovers from the big game party."

Emergency "What's for Dinner?" Plan

"What's for dinner?" is an age-old question that has been asked of home cooks for generations. All too often, it can put people in panic mode, especially as the clock on the kitchen wall ticks closer to the dinner hour.

By keeping boxes of Bisquick and other staple items on hand, though, meal preparation is easy—and enjoyable—even on the busiest of weeknights.

Bisquick Meals in Minutes

From pancakes or waffles in the morning to a potpie at dinner, Bisquick is your around-the-clock kitchen companion for simply delicious meals. Cooks from across the country love to share their favorite recipes that rely on Bisquick to turn out down-home dinners in a dash.

The "emergency" meal idea actually started on bettycrocker.com. Readers were asked to send their favorite emergency meal idea and found that Bisquick is a true hero when it comes to quick meals. The stories and quotes that accompanied the recipes are a true delight. When submitting her recipe for Macaroni and Cheese Pie (page 156), Anna of Illinois wrote, "Kids love it, and its quick! All it takes is Bisquick mix and some easy on-hand ingredients—it's dinner!"

A popular recipe is the Impossibly Easy Cheeseburger Pie (page 148). There are many great reasons to make this recipe but Rachelle of Arizona summed it up: "Whenever I'm stuck for

supper and I ask my husband what he really wants, he'll ask for Cheeseburger Pie." We also read this from Margie from Idaho: "Use lean sausage instead of the ground beef in the Cheeseburger Pie and serve it for breakfast." You can see how truly versatile Bisquick and these recipes are!

Plus, we love that Bisquick makes great pancakes and waffles. About the Apple Oven Pancake (page 35), Elaine from Kentucky said, "For breakfast, this is simply the easiest and best ever!"

So when you need a quick meal, be sure to turn to Bisquick and find your favorite emergency meal to brag about!

A Well-Stocked Pantry Saves the Day

One way to avoid a dinnertime crisis is by keeping your pantry supplied with everyday items that are often used in recipes and with convenience foods that give a head start to meal prep. Below is a basic list to get you started, but be sure to add your family's favorites as well.

- Bisquick Original, Heart Smart and Gluten Free mixes
- Baking supplies (baking soda and powder, flour, cornstarch, granulated and powdered sugar, nuts, shortening, vanilla extract and honey)
- Beans, peas and lentils (dried and canned)
- Canned meats and fish (chicken, tuna, salmon)
- Canned vegetables
- Old-fashioned or quick-cooking oats

- Condiments (jams/jellies, ketchup, mustard, mayonnaise, peanut butter, salsa)
- Dried herbs and spices
- Dry bread crumbs (plain and seasoned)
- Gravy (packets, jars and cans)
- Oils (canola, olive) and cooking spray
- Pasta and pasta sauce (various shapes and flavors, including dry pasta mixes)
- Rice (brown, instant, long grain, wild) and rice mixes

- Sauces (barbecue, soy, steak, Worcestershire, teriyaki, taco, hot pepper and tartar)
- Soups and broth (bouillon granules and canned soup)
- Syrups (maple syrup, light and dark corn syrup)
- Tomato products (crushed, diced, whole, paste, sauce and stewed)
- Vinegar (white, apple cider, balsamic and red wine)

Bisquick Goes Gluten-Free

What Is Celiac Disease?

Celiac disease is a digestive disorder affecting nearly 2 million Americans. For those suffering with the condition, it causes damage to the small intestine and interferes with nutrient absorption when foods containing protein glutens (found in barley, rye and wheat) are consumed. The only way to control celiac disease is through diet.

Tips for Gluten-Free Living

Unlike some other digestive conditions, there is no magic pill for curing celiac disease. The only way to manage it is by watching the foods you eat. At first, it may seem a little daunting. But with time, patience and planning, gluten-free cooking will soon become second nature.

If you are cooking gluten free, always read labels to make sure each recipe ingredient is gluten free. Products and ingredients can change.

- **Turn to others.** Once you're diagnosed with celiac disease, ask your doctor for resource information about how to live with the condition. Consider joining a support group online or in your community.

- **Shop the perimeter.** Purchase naturally gluten-free products by shopping for fresh produce, meat and dairy products. The more processed the food, the more likely it contains gluten proteins.

- **Pay attention in the aisles.** Grocery store shelves are loaded with products containing gluten, but gluten-free items are available. Do research online and in gluten-free cookbooks for the types of products you can and cannot eat. Keep the list with you while you shop.

- **Ask questions.** Many large supermarket chains offer printouts of the gluten-free products they carry. If you're unsure about an item, contact the manufacturer.

- **Read labels carefully.** Gluten proteins can appear in items you would never expect. Many websites provide lists of ingredients that are gluten-based.

- **Clean your kitchen.** Avoid cross-contamination by thoroughly washing utensils, cutting boards and other surfaces that have come in contact with foods containing gluten. Even the slightest bit of contact can trigger a reaction.

- **Learn how to eat out.** Research restaurants before going out to dinner because many chains are beginning to accommodate gluten-free diners. Whether you're at a dining establishment or at someone's home, ask questions about the food preparation before digging in.

Favorite Bisquick Gluten-Free Recipes

With Bisquick Gluten Free, people afflicted with celiac disease can now enjoy their favorite Bisquick recipes worry-free—without sacrificing flavor. Best of all, the whole family can delight in the dishes so cooks no longer need to make separate gluten-free foods for certain members of the family. Below are signature Bisquick recipes prepared with Bisquick Gluten Free mix. You'll find additional gluten-free dishes throughout the book.

Gluten Free Pancakes ● 10 pancakes

1 cup Bisquick Gluten Free mix
1 cup milk
2 tablespoons vegetable oil
1 egg

STIR ingredients until blended.
POUR slightly less than ¼ cupfuls onto hot greased griddle.
COOK until edges are dry. Turn; cook until golden.

Gluten Free Waffles ● 8 (4-inch) waffles

1⅓ cups Bisquick Gluten Free mix
1¼ cups milk
3 tablespoon vegetable oil
1 egg

STIR ingredients until blended.
POUR onto center of hot greased waffle maker; close lid
BAKE about 5 minutes or until steaming stops. Carefully remove waffle.

Gluten Free Biscuits ● 10 biscuits

2 cups Bisquick Gluten Free mix
⅓ cup shortening
⅔ cup milk
3 eggs

HEAT oven to 400°F.
CUT shortening into mix, using fork, until particles are size of small peas. Stir in remaining ingredients until soft dough forms.
DROP by spoonfuls onto ungreased cookie sheet, about 2 inches apart.
BAKE 13 to 16 minutes or until golden brown.

Gluten Free Pizza Crust • 6 servings

1⅓ cups Bisquick Gluten Free mix
½ teaspoon Italian seasoning or dried basil leaves
½ cup water
⅓ cup vegetable oil
2 eggs, beaten

EAT oven to 425°F. Grease 12-inch pizza pan with shortening or cooking spray.

STIR Bisquick mix, Italian seasoning, water, oil and eggs until well combined.

SPREAD dough in pan.

BAKE 15 minutes (crust will appear cracked).

Gluten Free Strawberry Shortcake • 6 servings

4 cups (1 quart) strawberries, sliced
½ cup sugar
2⅓ cups Bisquick Gluten Free mix
⅓ cup butter or margarine
¾ cup milk
½ teaspoon vanilla
3 eggs, beaten
¾ cup whipping cream, whipped

MIX strawberries and ¼ cup of the sugar; set aside.

HEAT oven to 425°F. Grease cookie sheet with shortening or cooking spray.

MIX Bisquick mix and remaining ¼ cup sugar. Using pastry blender (or pulling 2 knives through ingredients in opposite directions), cut in butter until mixture looks like crumbs. Stir in milk, vanilla and eggs.

DROP by 6 heaping spoonfuls onto cookie sheet, about 3 inches apart.

BAKE 10 to 12 minutes or until light golden brown. Cool 5 minutes. With serrated knife, split shortcakes; fill and top with strawberries and whipped cream.

CHAPTER 1

Breakfasts

and Brunches

Nutty Cereal Dollar Pancakes

PREP TIME: 25 MINUTES • START TO FINISH: 25 MINUTES

6 PANCAKES

¾ cup Wheaties® cereal, slightly crushed (½ cup)

¼ cup raisins

¼ cup dry-roasted sunflower nuts

2 cups Original Bisquick® mix

1½ cups Wheaties cereal, crushed (¾ cup)

1¼ cups milk

2 eggs

⅓ cup light fat-free creamy vanilla yogurt (or any flavor)

¾ cup honey

1 In small bowl, toss ½ cup slightly crushed cereal, raisins and nuts; set aside. In medium bowl, stir Bisquick mix, ¾ cup crushed cereal, milk and eggs with fork until blended.

2 Heat griddle to 375°F or 12-inch skillet over medium-high heat. (To test griddle, sprinkle with a few drops of water. If bubbles jump around, heat is just right.) Grease griddle with vegetable oil if necessary (or spray with cooking spray before heating).

3 For each pancake, pour 1 measuring tablespoon batter onto hot griddle. Cook until edges are dry. Turn; cook other sides until golden.

4 For each serving, arrange 6 pancakes on plate. Top with 1 tablespoon yogurt and 2½ tablespoons cereal mixture. Drizzle 2 tablespoons honey over all.

1 SERVING: Calories 450; Total Fat 12g (Saturated Fat 3g; Trans Fat 1g); Cholesterol 75mg; Sodium 750mg; Total Carbohydrate 79g (Dietary Fiber 2g); Protein 10g **Exchanges:** 3 Starch, 2 Other Carbohydrate, 2 Fat **Carbohydrate Choices:** 5

Quick Tip: You can vary this "emergency" breakfast to use what you have on hand. Instead of topping with the cereal mixture, try these mini pancakes with yogurt, honey, sliced strawberries or bananas.

Gluten Free Pancakes

PREP TIME: 20 MINUTES   START TO FINISH: 20 MINUTES

10 PANCAKES

1 cup Bisquick Gluten Free mix
1 cup milk
2 tablespoons vegetable oil
1 egg
Butter, if desired
Syrup, if desired

1 In large bowl, stir Bisquick mix, milk, oil and egg until well blended.

2 Heat griddle to 375°F or 12-inch skillet over medium-high heat. (To test griddle, sprinkle with a few drops of water. If bubbles jump around, heat is just right.) Grease griddle with vegetable oil if necessary (or spray with cooking spray before heating).

3 For each pancake, pour slightly less than ¼ cupful batter onto hot griddle. Cook pancakes until dry around edges. Turn; cook other sides until golden brown. Serve pancakes with butter and syrup, if desired.

1 PANCAKE: Calories 90; Total Fat 4g (Saturated Fat 1g; Trans Fat 0g); Cholesterol 25mg; Sodium 150mg; Total Carbohydrate 11g (Dietary Fiber 0g); Protein 2g **Exchanges:** 1 Starch, ½ Fat **Carbohydrate Choices:** 1

Quick Tip: For a healthier option, substitute your favorite fresh fruit for the syrup.

Quick Tip: Cooking gluten-free? Always read labels to make sure each recipe ingredient is gluten-free. Products and ingredient sources can change.

Oatmeal Pancakes with Banana-Walnut Syrup

PREP TIME: 30 MINUTES • **START TO FINISH: 30 MINUTES**

6 SERVINGS (3 PANCAKES EACH)

SYRUP

2 tablespoons butter or margarine

¼ cup chopped walnuts

2 bananas, sliced

1 cup maple-flavored syrup

PANCAKES

2 cups Original Bisquick mix

½ cup old-fashioned or quick-cooking oats

2 tablespoons packed brown sugar

1¼ cups milk

2 eggs

1 In 1½-quart saucepan, melt butter over medium heat. Add walnuts; cook, stirring occasionally, until walnuts and butter just begin to brown. Add bananas; stir to coat with butter. Stir in syrup. Reduce heat to low; cook until warm. Keep warm while making pancakes.

2 In medium bowl, stir pancake ingredients with whisk or fork until blended.

3 Heat griddle to 375°F or 12-inch skillet over medium-high heat. (To test griddle, sprinkle with a few drops of water. If bubbles jump around, heat is just right.) Grease griddle with vegetable oil if necessary (or spray with cooking spray before heating).

4 For each pancake, pour slightly less than ¼ cup batter onto hot griddle. Cook until edges are dry. Turn; cook other sides until golden brown. Serve with warm syrup.

1 SERVING: Calories 520; Total Fat 15g (Saturated Fat 6g; Trans Fat 1.5g); Cholesterol 85mg; Sodium 590mg; Total Carbohydrate 87g (Dietary Fiber 3g); Protein 9g **Exchanges:** 3 Starch, ½ Fruit, 2½ Other Carbohydrate, 2½ Fat **Carbohydrate Choices:** 6

Quick Tip: If you've got pecans on hand and not walnuts, go ahead and substitute them. Also, the butter can burn quickly, so watch it carefully while it's browning. It should be an even golden brown color.

Candied Ginger Pumpkin Pancakes

PREP TIME: 30 MINUTES   START TO FINISH: 30 MINUTES

16 PANCAKES

2 cups Original Bisquick mix

2 teaspoons pumpkin pie spice

1½ cups buttermilk

1 cup canned pumpkin (not pumpkin pie mix)

2 eggs

¼ cup toasted pecan halves, finely chopped*

1 tablespoon finely chopped crystallized ginger

Pecan halves, if desired

Butter, if desired

Maple-flavored syrup, if desired

1 In large bowl, stir Bisquick mix, pumpkin pie spice, buttermilk, pumpkin and eggs with whisk or fork until blended. Stir in chopped pecans and ginger.

2 Heat griddle to 375°F or 12-inch skillet over medium-high heat. (To test griddle, sprinkle with a few drops of water. If bubbles jump around, heat is just right.) Grease griddle with vegetable oil if necessary (or spray with cooking spray before heating).

3 For each pancake, pour slightly less than ¼ cup batter onto hot griddle. Cook until edges are dry. Turn; cook other sides until golden brown. Serve topped with remaining ingredients.

*To toast pecans, sprinkle in ungreased heavy skillet. Cook over medium heat 5 to 7 minutes, stirring frequently until pecans begin to brown, then stirring constantly until light brown.

1 PANCAKE: Calories 110; Total Fat 4.5g (Saturated Fat 1g; Trans Fat 0.5g); Cholesterol 30mg; Sodium 210mg; Total Carbohydrate 14g (Dietary Fiber 1g); Protein 3g **Exchanges:** 1 Starch, 1 Fat **Carbohydrate Choices:** 1

Quick Tip: If you don't have pumpkin pie spice, you can use 1 teaspoon ground cinnamon and ½ teaspoon each of ground nutmeg and ground ginger instead.

Double-Chocolate Strawberry Pancakes

PREP TIME: 40 MINUTES   START TO FINISH: 40 MINUTES

5 SERVINGS (3 PANCAKES EACH)

1½ cups Original Bisquick mix

¼ cup unsweetened baking cocoa

1 container (8 oz) sour cream

½ cup milk

2 teaspoons strawberry extract or vanilla

2 eggs

1 cup semisweet chocolate chips (6 oz)

Whipped cream or frozen (thawed) whipped topping

2 cups sliced fresh strawberries

Strawberry syrup

1 In large bowl, lightly stir Bisquick mix, cocoa, sour cream, milk, extract and eggs (do not overbeat; mixture should be lumpy). Fold in chocolate chips.

2 Heat griddle to 375°F or 12-inch skillet over medium-high heat. (To test griddle, sprinkle with a few drops of water. If bubbles jump around, heat is just right.) Grease griddle with vegetable oil if necessary (or spray with cooking spray before heating).

3 For each pancake, pour slightly less than ¼ cup batter onto hot griddle; spread batter with rubber spatula to 4 inches in diameter. Cook pancakes until bubbly on top, puffed and dry around edges, about 2 minutes. Turn; cook other sides until golden brown, about 1 to 2 minutes longer. Top with whipped cream, strawberries and syrup.

1 SERVING: Calories 510; Total Fat 27g (Saturated Fat 14g; Trans Fat 1.5g); Cholesterol 110mg; Sodium 520mg; Total Carbohydrate 55g (Dietary Fiber 5g); Protein 9g **Exchanges:** 1 Starch, 1 Fruit, 1½ Other Carbohydrate, 1 High-Fat Meat, 4 Fat **Carbohydrate Choices:** 3½

BETTER WITH BISQUICK

Contest Winner:

Joni Hilton • Rocklin, CA

This decadent dessert won 1st place in our Better with Bisquick Contest.

This is a true flavor blast of chocolate and strawberry—double doses of each! Everyone loves chocolate-dipped strawberries, so I thought a pancake combining those yummy flavors would be a real hit.

Gluten Free Waffles

PREP TIME: 20 MINUTES   START TO FINISH: 20 MINUTES

8 (4-INCH) WAFFLES

1⅓ cups Bisquick Gluten
    Free mix

1¼ cups milk

3 tablespoons vegetable oil

1 egg

Butter, if desired

Peach preserves, if desired

1 Heat waffle maker. (Waffle makers without a nonstick coating may need to be brushed with vegetable oil or sprayed with cooking spray.) In large bowl, stir Bisquick mix, milk, oil and egg with whisk or fork until blended.

2 Pour about ½ cup batter onto center of hot waffle maker. (Check manufacturer's directions for recommended amount of batter.) Close lid. Bake about 5 minutes or until steaming stops. Carefully remove waffle. Repeat with remaining batter. Serve with butter and peach preserves.

1 WAFFLE: Calories 150; Total Fat 7g (Saturated Fat 1.5g; Trans Fat 0g); Cholesterol 30mg; Sodium 250mg; Total Carbohydrate 19g (Dietary Fiber 0g); Protein 3g **Exchanges:** 1 Starch, 1½ Fat **Carbohydrate Choices:** 1

Quick Tip: Waffles can be served with syrup or any fresh fruit instead of peach preserves.

Peanut Butter Waffle Toast

PREP TIME: 20 MINUTES ▦ START TO FINISH: 20 MINUTES

6 TO 8 SERVINGS

1 cup Original Bisquick mix

2 tablespoons granulated sugar

1¼ cups milk

½ cup peanut butter

1 teaspoon vanilla

1 egg

6 to 8 slices bread

6 to 8 tablespoons miniature semisweet chocolate chips

Powdered sugar, if desired

1 Heat waffle maker. (Waffle makers without nonstick coating may need to be brushed with vegetable oil or sprayed with cooking spray.)

2 In medium bowl, stir Bisquick mix, granulated sugar, milk, peanut butter, vanilla and egg with whisk or fork until well blended. Carefully dip bread into batter on both sides. Place in hot waffle maker; close lid.

3 Bake about 2 minutes or until steaming stops and "toast" is golden. Carefully remove waffle toast. Sprinkle each waffle with 1 tablespoon chocolate chips and powdered sugar.

1 SERVING: Calories 400; Total Fat 20g (Saturated Fat 6g; Trans Fat 0.5g); Cholesterol 40mg; Sodium 550mg; Total Carbohydrate 43g (Dietary Fiber 3g); Protein 12g **Exchanges:** 1½ Starch, 1½ Other Carbohydrate, 1 High-Fat Meat, 2 Fat **Carbohydrate Choices:** 3

Quick Tip: The peanutty batter covering the bread is thick so it clings to the bread. If it seems a little too thick, add a small amount of milk. When you coat the bread, use your fingers or a spatula to turn the slices. Either way, the toast turns out delicious!

Cream Cheese–Filled Batter-Dipped French Toast

PREP TIME: 35 MINUTES ▪ **START TO FINISH: 35 MINUTES**

8 SERVINGS

5 oz cream cheese, softened

¼ cup orange marmalade

16 diagonally cut slices (½ inch thick) French bread

1 cup Original Bisquick mix

1 teaspoon ground cinnamon

½ teaspoon grated orange peel

⅔ cup milk

½ teaspoon vanilla

1 egg

1 tablespoon powdered sugar

Maple-flavored syrup, if desired

1 In small bowl, mix cream cheese and marmalade until blended. Spread 8 slices of the bread with cream cheese mixture. Top each with 1 of the remaining bread slices, making 8 sandwiches.

2 In shallow dish or pie pan, stir Bisquick mix, cinnamon, orange peel, milk, vanilla and egg with whisk or fork until blended.

3 Heat nonstick griddle to 350°F or nonstick skillet over medium heat. Dip each sandwich into batter mixture, turning to coat both sides; drain excess batter in dish. Cook on hot griddle or skillet 1 to 2 minutes on each side or until golden brown. Sprinkle each sandwich with powdered sugar; serve with syrup.

1 SERVING: Calories 550; Total Fat 11g (Saturated Fat 5g; Trans Fat 1g); Cholesterol 50mg; Sodium 1090mg; Total Carbohydrate 92g (Dietary Fiber 4g); Protein 18g **Exchanges:** 4 Starch, 1½ Other Carbohydrate, ½ Milk, 1 Fat **Carbohydrate Choices:** 6

Quick Tip: For an easy substitution, use English muffin bread or swirled cinnamon bread in place of the French bread.

Baked Apple Breakfast Wedges

PREP TIME: 15 MINUTES ▪ **START TO FINISH: 40 MINUTES**

6 SERVINGS

¼ **cup packed brown sugar**

¼ **teaspoon ground cinnamon**

2 **medium cooking apples, peeled, thinly sliced (about 2 cups)**

⅓ **cup water**

2 **tablespoons butter or margarine**

½ **cup Original Bisquick mix**

2 **eggs**

Maple-flavored syrup, if desired

1 Heat oven to 400°F. Generously grease 9-inch glass pie plate with shortening or cooking spray. In medium bowl, mix brown sugar and cinnamon. Add apples; toss and set aside.

2 In 2-quart saucepan, heat water and butter to boiling. Reduce heat to low. Add Bisquick mix; stir vigorously until mixture forms a ball. Remove from heat. Beat in eggs, one at a time, beating until smooth.

3 Spread batter across bottom and sides of pie plate. Arrange apples on top to within 1 inch of edge of pie plate.

4 Bake about 23 minutes or until puffed and edges are golden brown. Serve immediately. Drizzle with syrup.

1 SERVING: Calories 160; Total Fat 7g (Saturated Fat 3.5g; Trans Fat 0.5g); Cholesterol 80mg; Sodium 170mg; Total Carbohydrate 20g (Dietary Fiber 0g); Protein 3g **Exchanges:** 1 Starch, ½ Other Carbohydrate, 1 Fat **Carbohydrate Choices:** 1

Quick Tip: For a special touch, sprinkle with powdered sugar and serve with warm maple syrup.

Apple Oven Pancake

PREP TIME: 25 MINUTES ▦ **START TO FINISH: 55 MINUTES**

8 SERVINGS

3 tablespoons butter or
   margarine

4 medium cooking apples,
   peeled, thinly sliced
   (about 6 cups)

¼ cup packed brown sugar

2 teaspoons ground cinnamon

1½ cups Original Bisquick mix

¼ cup granulated sugar

1 cup buttermilk

1 tablespoon fresh lemon juice

1 teaspoon vanilla

2 eggs

1 tablespoon cinnamon-sugar

Maple-flavored syrup,
   if desired

1 Heat oven to 450°F. In 10-inch ovenproof or cast-iron skillet, melt butter in oven about 2 minutes. Add apples, brown sugar and cinnamon; toss to coat apples. (Pan will be very hot.) Bake 2 minutes longer. Stir; bake 3 minutes longer. Stir again. Reduce oven temperature to 400°F.

2 In large bowl, beat Bisquick mix, granulated sugar, buttermilk, lemon juice, vanilla and eggs with whisk or fork until blended. Pour over apples.

3 Bake 25 to 30 minutes or until golden brown. Sprinkle with cinnamon-sugar. Cut into wedges. Drizzle with syrup. Serve immediately.

1 SERVING: Calories 280; Total Fat 9g (Saturated Fat 4.5g; Trans Fat 1g); Cholesterol 65mg; Sodium 370mg; Total Carbohydrate 43g (Dietary Fiber 2g); Protein 5g **Exchanges:** 1 Starch, ½ Fruit, 1½ Other Carbohydrate, 1½ Fat **Carbohydrate Choices:** 3

Quick Tip: Peel the apples quickly with a vegetable peeler. Then use a very sharp knife to slice them. Remember that the best baking apples are slightly tart. Top choices are Braeburn, Granny Smith, Cortland, Northern Spy and Rome Beauty.

Puffed Pancake Brunch Casserole

PREP TIME: 15 MINUTES ■ START TO FINISH: 1 HOUR 5 MINUTES

10 SERVINGS

½ cup butter

2 cups Original Bisquick mix

2 cups milk

8 eggs

1 cup shredded Swiss cheese (4 oz)

1 lb cubed cooked ham (about 3 cups)

1 package (2.1 oz) precooked bacon, chopped

2 cups shredded Cheddar cheese (8 oz)

¼ teaspoon salt

¼ teaspoon ground mustard

Dash ground nutmeg

1 Heat oven to 375°F. Spray 13×9-inch (3-quart) glass baking dish with cooking spray. Place butter in dish; place in oven until melted, about 10 minutes.

2 In medium bowl, mix Bisquick mix, 1 cup of the milk and 2 of the eggs with whisk until tiny lumps remain. Pour over butter in baking dish. Layer with Swiss cheese, ham, bacon and Cheddar cheese.

3 In large bowl, mix remaining 1 cup milk, remaining 6 eggs, the salt, mustard and nutmeg. Pour over casserole.

4 Bake uncovered 35 to 40 minutes or until golden brown. Let stand 10 minutes before serving.

1 SERVING: Calories 510; Total Fat 34g (Saturated Fat 18g; Trans Fat 1.5g); Cholesterol 265mg; Sodium 1470mg; Total Carbohydrate 19g (Dietary Fiber 0g); Protein 29g **Exchanges:** 1½ Starch, 3½ High-Fat Meat, 1 Fat **Carbohydrate Choices:** 1

BETTER with BISQUICK

Contest Winner:

Heather Markowski • Valatie, NY

This recipe won honorable mention in our Better with Bisquick Contest.

"*Nothing slows down life and starts off a good day more than a good breakfast. We're a breakfast family. We love to sit down together and have breakfast. The aroma of breakfast cooking gets everyone going.*

Cheesy Vegetable Crepes

PREP TIME: 35 MINUTES ▪ START TO FINISH: 50 MINUTES

6 SERVINGS (2 CREPES EACH)

VEGETABLE FILLING

2 tablespoons vegetable oil

2 medium zucchini, coarsely chopped (3 to 4 cups)

$\frac{1}{2}$ cup chopped green bell pepper

4 medium green onions, sliced ($\frac{1}{4}$ cup)

$\frac{1}{4}$ teaspoon dried minced garlic

2 medium tomatoes, coarsely chopped (1$\frac{1}{2}$ cups)

$\frac{1}{2}$ teaspoon salt

CREPES

1 cup Original Bisquick mix

$\frac{3}{4}$ cup milk

2 eggs

1 cup grated Parmesan cheese

1 In 10-inch skillet, heat oil over medium heat. Add zucchini, bell pepper, onions and garlic; cook 3 to 5 minutes, stirring occasionally, until vegetables are crisp-tender. Remove from heat; stir in tomatoes. Sprinkle with salt. Cover; let stand 2 to 3 minutes.

2 Lightly grease 6- or 7-inch skillet; heat over medium-high heat. In medium bowl, stir Bisquick mix, milk and eggs with whisk or fork until blended.

3 Heat oven to 350°F. For each crepe, pour 2 tablespoons batter into hot skillet; rotate skillet until batter covers bottom. Cook over medium-high heat until golden brown. Gently loosen edge with spatula; turn and cook other side until golden brown. Stack crepes, placing waxed paper between, as removed from skillet. Keep crepes covered to prevent drying out.

4 Spoon filling onto each crepe. Sprinkle half of cheese over filling on crepes. Roll up crepes; place seam sides down in ungreased 11×7-inch (2-quart) glass baking dish. Sprinkle with remaining cheese. Bake uncovered 10 to 12 minutes or until hot.

1 SERVING: Calories 260; Total Fat 15g (Saturated Fat 5g; Trans Fat 0.5g); Cholesterol 90mg; Sodium 780mg; Total Carbohydrate 19g (Dietary Fiber 2g); Protein 12g **Exchanges:** $\frac{1}{2}$ Starch, $\frac{1}{2}$ Other Carbohydrate, 1 Vegetable, 1 Medium-Fat Meat, 2 Fat **Carbohydrate Choices:** 1

Quick Tip: Crepes can be frozen up to 3 months. Stack cool, unfilled crepes with waxed paper between. Wrap in foil, or place in a resealable freezer plastic bag; label and freeze. Thaw at room temperature about 1 hour or in refrigerator 6 to 8 hours.

Rajin' Cajun Quiche

PREP TIME: 20 MINUTES ▪ **START TO FINISH: 1 HOUR**

6 SERVINGS

1¼ cups Original Bisquick mix

¼ cup butter or margarine, softened

2 tablespoons hot water

4 oz pepper Jack cheese, shredded

1 cup diced smoked spicy andouille sausage (about 6 oz)

⅓ cup thinly sliced green onions

1 cup half-and-half

1½ teaspoons Cajun seasoning

3 eggs

1 Heat oven to 400°F. Spray 9-inch glass pie plate with cooking spray. In medium bowl, stir Bisquick mix and butter until mixed. (Mixture will be crumbly.) Add hot water; stir until soft dough forms. Press dough in bottom and up side of pie plate.

2 Layer cheese, sausage and green onions over crust in pie plate. In medium bowl, beat half-and-half, Cajun seasoning and eggs with whisk or fork until blended. Pour into pie plate.

3 Bake 32 to 38 minutes or until knife inserted in center comes out clean. Let stand 10 minutes before serving.

1 SERVING: Calories 500; Total Fat 32g (Saturated Fat 16g; Trans Fat 1.5g); Cholesterol 240mg, Sodium 1330mg; Total Carbohydrate 24g (Dietary Fiber 1g); Protein 29g **Exchanges:** 1 Starch, ½ Low-Fat Milk, 3 Lean Meat, 4 Fat **Carbohydrate Choices:** 1½

Quick Tip: Look for spicy Cajun seasoning in the herb and spice section of your grocery store.

Southwest Tamale Tart

PREP TIME: 30 MINUTES ▪ **START TO FINISH: 1 HOUR 5 MINUTES**

6 SERVINGS

1¹⁄₂ cups reduced-fat shredded Cheddar cheese (6 oz)

1 cup Bisquick Heart Smart® mix

¹⁄₂ cup cornmeal

1 can (4.5 oz) chopped green chiles, drained

¹⁄₃ cup condensed beef broth

1 can (15 oz) black beans, drained, rinsed

¹⁄₂ cup chopped fresh cilantro

2 small tomatoes, seeded, chopped

Low-fat sour cream, if desired

Chunky-style salsa, if desired

1 Heat oven to 350°F. Spray 9-inch springform pan with cooking spray. In medium bowl, mix 1 cup of the cheese, the Bisquick mix, cornmeal and chiles. Stir in broth. Pat mixture evenly in bottom of pan.

2 In small bowl, mix beans and cilantro. Spoon over mixture in baking dish to within ¹⁄₂ inch of edge. Sprinkle with remaining cheese.

3 Bake 35 minutes. Run knife around edge of pan to loosen tart; remove side of pan. Arrange tomatoes around edge of tart. Cut into wedges; top with sour cream. Serve with salsa.

1 SERVING: Calories 240; Total Fat 4g (Saturated Fat 1.5g; Trans Fat 0g); Cholesterol 5mg; Sodium 860mg; Total Carbohydrate 37g (Dietary Fiber 4g); Protein 14g **Exchanges:** 2¹⁄₂ Starch, ¹⁄₂ Medium-Fat Meat **Carbohydrate Choices:** 2¹⁄₂

Quick Tip: If you have beef broth remaining, freeze it in a clean ice-cube tray. Store the frozen broth cubes in a resealable freezer plastic bag and use in soups and stews. Pull one out to add extra flavor to meat dishes.

Tomato-Pesto Brunch Bake

PREP TIME: 20 MINUTES ▪ **START TO FINISH: 1 HOUR 5 MINUTES**

12 SERVINGS

2 ½ cups Original Bisquick mix

½ cup grated Parmesan cheese

¾ cup milk

2 cups shredded mozzarella cheese (8 oz)

3 large tomatoes, cut into thin slices

½ cup refrigerated basil pesto

4 eggs

½ cup whipping cream

1 teaspoon salt

½ teaspoon white pepper

1 Heat oven to 350°F. In medium bowl, stir Bisquick mix, Parmesan cheese and milk until soft dough forms. With fingers dipped in Bisquick mix, press dough in bottom and ½ inch up sides of ungreased 13×9-inch (3-quart) glass baking dish.

2 Sprinkle 1½ cups of the mozzarella cheese over crust. Layer tomatoes over cheese, overlapping if necessary. Spread pesto over tomatoes.

3 In medium bowl, beat eggs, whipping cream, salt and pepper with whisk or fork until blended. Gently pour mixture over tomatoes. Sprinkle with remaining ½ cup mozzarella cheese.

4 Bake 35 to 40 minutes or until top is golden brown. Let stand 5 minutes before serving.

1 SERVING: Calories 300; Total Fat 19g (Saturated Fat 8g; Trans Fat 1g); Cholesterol 100mg; Sodium 780mg; Total Carbohydrate 21g (Dietary Fiber 1g); Protein 12g **Exchanges:** 1 Starch, ½ Low-Fat Milk, ½ Vegetable, ½ Lean Meat, 3 Fat **Carbohydrate Choices:** 1½

Quick Tip: The standing time for this dish, like many egg-based dishes, allows it to set before being cut.

Garden Veggie Bake

PREP TIME: 15 MINUTES   **START TO FINISH: 55 MINUTES**

4 SERVINGS

1 cup chopped zucchini

1 large tomato, chopped (1 cup)

1 medium onion, chopped ($^1/_2$ cup)

$^1/_3$ cup grated Parmesan cheese

$^1/_2$ cup Bisquick Heart Smart mix

1 cup fat-free (skim) milk

$^1/_2$ cup fat-free egg product or 2 eggs

$^1/_2$ teaspoon salt

$^1/_8$ teaspoon pepper

1 Heat oven to 400°F. Lightly spray 8-inch square (2-quart) glass baking dish or 9-inch glass pie plate with cooking spray. Sprinkle zucchini, tomato, onion and cheese in baking dish.

2 In medium bowl, stir remaining ingredients with whisk or fork until blended. Pour over vegetables and cheese.

3 Bake uncovered about 35 minutes or until knife inserted in center comes out clean. Cool 5 minutes before serving.

1 SERVING: Calories 150; Total Fat 3.5g (Saturated Fat 1.5g; Trans Fat 0g); Cholesterol 10mg; Sodium 640mg; Total Carbohydrate 19g (Dietary Fiber 1g); Protein 10g **Exchanges:** 1 Starch, 1 Vegetable, $^1/_2$ Lean Meat **Carbohydrate Choices:** 1

Quick Tip: Chopped bell peppers can be substituted for all or part of the zucchini.

Vegetable-Cheese Strata

PREP TIME: 15 MINUTES ▪ START TO FINISH: 4 HOURS 40 MINUTES

8 SERVINGS

1⅔ cups Original Bisquick mix

3 tablespoons Italian dressing

3 tablespoons milk

1 bag (1 lb) frozen broccoli, green beans, pearl onions and red peppers (or other combination), thawed, drained

8 eggs

3 cups milk

1 teaspoon yellow mustard

½ teaspoon seasoned salt

¼ teaspoon pepper

2 cups shredded Cheddar cheese (8 oz)

1 Heat oven to 450°F. Generously spray 13×9-inch (3-quart) glass baking dish with cooking spray. In medium bowl, stir Bisquick mix, Italian dressing and 3 tablespoons milk until soft dough forms. Pat dough in bottom of baking dish. Bake 8 minutes. Cool completely, about 45 minutes.

2 Sprinkle vegetables over baked crust. In medium bowl, beat all remaining ingredients except cheese with whisk or fork until blended. Pour over vegetables. Sprinkle with cheese. Cover; refrigerate at least 2 hours.

3 Heat oven to 350°F. Cover with foil; bake 30 minutes. Uncover dish; bake 40 to 50 minutes longer or until knife inserted in center comes out clean. Let stand 10 minutes.

1 SERVING: Calories 370; Total Fat 21g (Saturated Fat 10g; Trans Fat 1.5g); Cholesterol 250mg; Sodium 780mg; Total Carbohydrate 25g (Dietary Fiber 2g); Protein 20g **Exchanges:** 1 Starch, 2 Vegetable, 2 Medium-Fat Meat, 2 Fat **Carbohydrate Choices:** 1½

Quick Tip: It's nice when you can substitute what you have on hand instead of running out for another ingredient. You can use French, ranch or honey-mustard dressing in place of the Italian dressing. Also Colby would be a tasty and quick substitute for the Cheddar cheese.

Cheesy Sausage and Egg Bake

PREP TIME: 25 MINUTES ▪ **START TO FINISH: 1 HOUR**

12 SERVINGS

1 lb bulk pork sausage, cooked, drained

1½ cups sliced fresh mushrooms (4 oz)

8 medium green onions, sliced (½ cup)

2 medium tomatoes, chopped (1½ cups)

2 cups shredded mozzarella cheese (8 oz)

1¼ cups Original Bisquick mix

1½ teaspoons salt

1½ teaspoons chopped fresh or ½ teaspoon dried oregano leaves

½ teaspoon pepper

1 cup milk

12 eggs

1 Heat oven to 350°F. Spray 13×9-inch (3-quart) glass baking dish with cooking spray. Layer sausage, mushrooms, onions, tomatoes and cheese in baking dish.

2 In medium bowl, stir remaining ingredients with whisk or fork until blended. Pour over cheese.

3 Bake uncovered 30 to 35 minutes or until golden brown and set.

1 SERVING: Calories 260; Total Fat 16g (Saturated Fat 6g; Trans Fat 0.5g); Cholesterol 240mg; Sodium 750mg; Total Carbohydrate 12g (Dietary Fiber 0g); Protein 17g **Exchanges:** 1 Starch, 2 High-Fat Meat **Carbohydrate Choices:** 1

Quick Tip: Having guests and want to do some prep ahead of time? Cook the sausage and layer with mushrooms, onions, tomatoes and cheese in the baking dish. Cover and refrigerate. Just before baking, pour the Bisquick mixture over the top.

Sausage and Cheese Breakfast Torte

PREP TIME: 30 MINUTES ▪ START TO FINISH: 40 MINUTES

10 SERVINGS

1 cup Original Bisquick mix

¹⁄₂ cup yellow cornmeal

2 cups shredded extra-sharp Cheddar cheese (8 oz)

¹⁄₂ cup reduced-sodium chicken broth or water

4 slices applewood-smoked thick-sliced bacon, cut into bite-size pieces

¹⁄₂ lb bulk pork sausage

8 eggs

¹⁄₄ cup half-and-half

¹⁄₂ teaspoon freeze-dried chopped chives

¹⁄₈ teaspoon salt

1 tablespoon butter

¹⁄₃ cup crumbled peppercorn feta or plain feta cheese

1 Heat oven to 350°F. Spray 10-inch springform pan with cooking spray. In medium bowl, mix Bisquick mix, cornmeal and 1 cup of the Cheddar cheese. Stir in broth until blended. Using greased or buttered hands, press mixture in bottom of pan to form crust.

2 Bake 20 minutes or until crust is set and beginning to brown around edges.

3 Meanwhile, in 12-inch nonstick skillet, cook bacon, stirring frequently, until crisp. Remove bacon to paper towels; set aside. Discard bacon drippings from skillet. In same skillet, cook sausage over medium heat, stirring frequently, until no longer pink. Remove sausage to bowl.

4 In large bowl, beat eggs, half-and-half, chives and salt with whisk or fork. In same skillet, melt butter over medium heat. Add egg mixture; cook and stir until eggs are just moist (not dry). Remove from heat; stir in sausage and feta cheese. Spread mixture evenly over crust. Sprinkle with remaining 1 cup Cheddar cheese and the bacon.

5 Bake 8 to 10 minutes or until thoroughly heated and cheese is melted. Run metal spatula or table knife along side of torte to loosen from pan; remove side of pan. Cut into wedges; serve immediately.

1 SERVING: Calories 320; Total Fat 21g (Saturated Fat 10g; Trans Fat 1g); Cholesterol 215mg; Sodium 650mg; Total Carbohydrate 15g (Dietary Fiber 0g); Protein 17g **Exchanges:** 1 Starch, 2 High-Fat Meat, 1 Fat **Carbohydrate Choices:** 1

BETTER WITH BISQUICK

Contest Winner:

**Barbara Estabrook •
Rhinelander, WI**

This recipe won honorable mention in our Better with Bisquick Contest.

This breakfast or brunch torte is like a deep-dish breakfast pizza, but instead of a pizza pan, I found a springform pan works best.

Gluten Free Impossibly Easy Breakfast Bake

PREP TIME: 20 MINUTES ⬦ **START TO FINISH: 1 HOUR 5 MINUTES**

12 SERVINGS

1 package (16 oz) bulk pork sausage

1 medium red bell pepper, chopped

1 medium onion, chopped (¹⁄₂ cup)

3 cups frozen hash brown potatoes

2 cups shredded Cheddar cheese (8 oz)

³⁄₄ cup Bisquick Gluten Free mix

¹⁄₄ teaspoon pepper

2 cups milk

6 eggs

1 Heat oven to 400°F. Spray 13×9-inch (3-quart) glass baking dish with cooking spray. In 10-inch skillet, cook sausage, bell pepper and onion over medium heat, stirring occasionally, until sausage is no longer pink; drain. In baking dish, mix sausage mixture, potatoes and 1½ cups of the cheese.

2 In medium bowl, stir Bisquick mix, pepper, milk and eggs with whisk or fork until blended. Pour over sausage mixture in baking dish.

3 Bake 30 to 35 minutes or until knife inserted in center comes out clean. Sprinkle with remaining ½ cup cheese; bake about 3 minutes longer or until cheese is melted. Let stand 5 minutes before serving.

1 SERVING: Calories 270; Total Fat 15g (Saturated Fat 7g; Trans Fat 0g); Cholesterol 145mg; Sodium 520mg; Total Carbohydrate 21g (Dietary Fiber 1g); Protein 14g **Exchanges:** 1 Starch, 1 Vegetable, 1 High-Fat Meat, 1¹⁄₂ Fat **Carbohydrate Choices:** 1¹⁄₂

Quick Tip: Frozen hash brown potatoes are great to have on hand for easy dishes like this.

Smoked Salmon Breakfast Squares

PREP TIME: 20 MINUTES ▪ **START TO FINISH: 5 HOURS 10 MINUTES**

12 SERVINGS

2 boxes (5.2 oz each) seasoned hash brown potato mix for skillets

1 package (8 oz) cream cheese, cut into $\frac{1}{2}$-inch cubes

6 oz smoked salmon, flaked

1 tablespoon dried chopped onion

1 cup Original Bisquick mix

$\frac{1}{2}$ teaspoon pepper

3 cups milk

4 eggs

4 oz pepper Jack cheese, shredded

$\frac{1}{2}$ cup chopped green onion tops (green part only)

1 Spray 13×9-inch (3-quart) glass baking dish with cooking spray. Sprinkle 1 box potatoes in baking dish. Place half of the cream cheese cubes and the salmon pieces over potatoes. Sprinkle with dried onion. Top with remaining box of potatoes and cream cheese.

2 In large bowl, beat Bisquick mix, pepper, milk and eggs with whisk or fork until blended. Pour over mixture in baking dish. Sprinkle with shredded cheese. Cover with foil; refrigerate at least 4 hours but no longer than 24 hours.

3 Heat oven to 375°F. Bake uncovered 32 to 38 minutes or until golden brown and knife inserted in center comes out clean. Sprinkle with green onions. Let stand 10 minutes before serving.

1 SERVING: Calories 300; Total Fat 14g (Saturated Fat 7g; Trans Fat 0.5g); Cholesterol 110mg; Sodium 830mg; Total Carbohydrate 29g (Dietary Fiber 2g); Protein 12g **Exchanges:** 2 Starch, 1 Lean Meat, 2 Fat **Carbohydrate Choices:** 2

Quick Tip: Serve this make-ahead breakfast dish with toasted mini bagels and fresh fruit.

CHAPTER 2

Small Bites

and Simple Snacks

Apricot-Glazed Coconut-Chicken Bites

PREP TIME: 15 MINUTES ● START TO FINISH: 50 MINUTES
ABOUT 3 DOZEN APPETIZERS

¹⁄₄ **cup butter or margarine, melted**

¹⁄₂ **cup sweetened condensed milk**

4 tablespoons Dijon mustard

1¹⁄₂ **cups Original Bisquick mix**

²⁄₃ **cup flaked coconut**

¹⁄₂ **teaspoon salt**

¹⁄₂ **teaspoon paprika**

1 lb boneless skinless chicken breasts, cut into 1-inch pieces

¹⁄₂ **cup apricot spreadable fruit**

2 tablespoons honey

1 tablespoon white vinegar

Hot mustard, if desired

1 Heat oven to 425°F. Spread 2 tablespoons of the butter in 15×10×1-inch pan.

2 In shallow dish, mix sweetened condensed milk and 2 tablespoons of the Dijon mustard. In another shallow dish, mix Bisquick mix, coconut, salt and paprika. Dip chicken into milk mixture, then coat with Bisquick mixture. Place coated chicken in pan. Drizzle remaining butter over chicken.

3 Bake uncovered 12 minutes. Meanwhile, in small bowl, stir together spreadable fruit, honey, remaining 2 tablespoons Dijon mustard and the vinegar.

4 Turn chicken; brush with apricot mixture. Bake 7 to 8 minutes longer or until chicken is no longer pink in center and glaze is bubbly. Serve with hot mustard.

1 APPETIZER: Calories 90; Total Fat 4g (Saturated Fat 2g; Trans Fat 0g); Cholesterol 15mg; Sodium 160mg; Total Carbohydrate 10g (Dietary Fiber 0g); Protein 3g **Exchanges:** 1 Starch, ¹⁄₂ Fat **Carbohydrate Choices:** ¹⁄₂

Quick Tip: Simplify cleanup by lining your pan with foil before spreading butter in the pan.

Mini Chinese Chicken Snacks

PREP TIME: 25 MINUTES   START TO FINISH: 50 MINUTES
2 DOZEN APPETIZERS

CUPS

1¼ cups Original Bisquick mix

**¼ cup butter or
  margarine, softened**

2 tablespoons boiling water

FILLING

1 egg

½ cup half-and-half

⅓ cup finely shredded carrot

**⅓ cup drained sliced
  water chestnuts (from
  8-oz can), chopped**

1 tablespoon grated lemon peel

½ teaspoon salt

½ teaspoon garlic powder

½ teaspoon five-spice powder

**1 medium green onion, thinly
  sliced (1 tablespoon)**

**1 can (5 oz) chunk
  chicken, drained**

1 Heat oven to 375°F. Generously grease 24 mini muffin cups with shortening or cooking spray. In small bowl, stir Bisquick mix and butter until blended. Add boiling water; stir vigorously until soft dough forms. Press rounded teaspoonful of dough in bottom and up side of each cup.

2 In medium bowl, beat egg and half-and-half. Stir in remaining filling ingredients. Spoon about 1 tablespoon mixture into each cup.

3 Bake 20 to 25 minutes or until edges are golden brown and centers are set. Serve warm. Store covered in refrigerator.

1 APPETIZER: Calories 60; Total Fat 3.5g (Saturated Fat 2g; Trans Fat 0g); Cholesterol 20mg; Sodium 170mg; Total Carbohydrate 5g (Dietary Fiber 0g); Protein 2g **Exchanges:** ½ Starch, ½ Fat **Carbohydrate Choices:** ½

Quick Tip: For a pretty presentation, sprinkle tops of appetizers with chopped peanuts, chopped fresh cilantro or green onions just before serving.

Sesame Pork Strips

PREP TIME: 15 MINUTES   START TO FINISH: 45 MINUTES
ABOUT 3 DOZEN APPETIZERS

1 tablespoon butter or
    margarine, melted

1 lb boneless pork loin chops,
    1 inch thick

1¼ cups Original Bisquick mix

⅓ cup sesame seed

1 teaspoon salt

1 teaspoon ground mustard

1 teaspoon paprika

2 eggs

2 tablespoons milk

2 tablespoons butter or
    margarine, melted

Sweet-and-sour sauce or
    mustard, if desired

1 Heat oven to 400°F. Spread 1 tablespoon butter in 15×10×1-inch pan. Remove fat from pork. Cut pork into ¼-inch slices; cut slices into ½-inch wide strips.

2 In medium shallow dish, mix Bisquick, sesame seed, salt, mustard and paprika. In small shallow dish, beat eggs and milk with fork. Dip pork strips into egg mixture, then coat with Bisquick mixture. Place in single layer in pan. Drizzle 2 tablespoons butter over pork.

3 Bake 25 to 30 minutes or until brown and crisp. Serve with sweet-and-sour sauce.

1 APPETIZER: Calories 50, Total Fat 3g (Saturated Fat 1g; Trans Fat 0g); Cholesterol 20mg; Sodium 135mg; Total Carbohydrate 3g (Dietary Fiber 0g); Protein 3g **Exchanges:** ½ Medium-Fat Meat **Carbohydrate Choices:** 0

Quick Tip: This sesame coating is equally delicious on chicken. To make sesame chicken strips, substitute 1 pound boneless chicken breasts for the pork.

Crab Mini-Quiches

1¼ cups Original Bisquick mix

¼ cup butter or margarine, softened

2 tablespoons boiling water

⅓ cup canned crabmeat, finely chopped cooked crabmeat or finely chopped imitation crabmeat

½ cup half-and-half

1 egg

2 medium green onions, thinly sliced (2 tablespoons)

¼ teaspoon salt

¼ teaspoon ground red pepper (cayenne)

½ cup shredded Parmesan cheese

1 Heat oven to 375°F. Spray 24 small muffin cups, 1¾×1-inch, with cooking spray. Stir Bisquick mix and butter in small bowl until blended. Add boiling water; stir vigorously until soft dough forms. Press rounded teaspoonful of dough on bottom and up side of each muffin cup. Divide crabmeat evenly among muffin cups.

2 Beat half-and-half and egg in small bowl with spoon until blended. Stir in onions, salt and red pepper. Spoon 1½ teaspoons egg mixture into each muffin cup. Sprinkle cheese over tops.

3 Bake about 20 minutes or until edges are golden brown and centers are set. Cool 5 minutes. Loosen sides of quiches from pan; remove from pan.

1 MINI-QUICHE: Calories 60; Total Fat 4g (Saturated Fat 2.5g, Trans Fat 0g); Cholesterol 20mg; Sodium 160mg; Total Carbohydrate 5g (Dietary Fiber 0g); Protein 2g **Exchanges:** ½ Starch, ½ Fat **Carbohydrate Choices:** ½

Quick Tip: To make one day ahead, after baking, remove quiches from muffin pan and place on wire rack to cool. Cover; refrigerate. To serve, place on cookie sheet; cover loosely with foil. Bake at 375°F 9 to 11 minutes or until hot.

Gluten Free Sausage Cheese Balls

$^3/_4$ **cup Bisquick Gluten Free mix**

4 oz bulk pork sausage

1$^1/_2$ cups shredded Cheddar cheese (6 oz)

$^1/_4$ **cup grated Parmesan cheese**

$^1/_4$ **teaspoon garlic powder**

$^1/_4$ **teaspoon dried rosemary leaves, crushed**

$^1/_8$ **teaspoon ground red pepper (cayenne)**

$^1/_2$ **cup milk**

2 tablespoons chopped fresh parsley

Barbecue sauce or chili sauce, if desired

1 Heat oven to 350°F. Spray 15×10×1-inch pan with cooking spray. In large bowl, mix all ingredients except barbecue sauce. Shape mixture into 1-inch balls. Place in pan.

2 Bake uncovered 22 to 26 minutes or until light golden brown. Immediately remove from pan. Serve warm with barbecue sauce for dipping.

1 SERVING: Calories 30; Total Fat 1.5g (Saturated Fat 1g; Trans Fat 0g); Cholesterol 5mg; Sodium 60mg; Total Carbohydrate 2g (Dietary Fiber 0g); Protein 1g **Exchanges:** $^1/_2$ Fat **Carbohydrate Choices:** 0

Quick Tip: You can use turkey sausage as a substitute for the pork sausage.

Pesto and Cheese Pizza

PREP TIME: 20 MINUTES • START TO FINISH: 45 MINUTES
8 SERVINGS

CRUST

3 cups Original Bisquick mix

²/₃ cup very hot water

2 tablespoons olive or vegetable oil

4 sticks (1 oz each) mozzarella string cheese, cut in half lengthwise

TOPPINGS

¹/₃ cup refrigerated basil pesto (from 7-oz container)

1 bag (7 oz) shredded mozzarella cheese with sun-dried tomatoes and basil or plain mozzarella cheese (1³/₄ cups)

1¹/₂ cups yellow, red and green bell pepper strips (¹/₈ inch)

1 Move oven rack to lowest position. Heat oven to 450°F. Spray 12-inch pizza pan with cooking spray. In large bowl, stir Bisquick mix, water and oil with fork until soft dough forms; beat vigorously 20 strokes. Cover; let stand 8 minutes.

2 Pat or press dough in bottom and 1 inch over side of pizza pan. Place string cheese along edge of dough, overlapping if necessary. Fold 1-inch edge of dough over and around cheese; press to seal.

3 Bake 6 to 7 minutes or until lightly browned around edges.

4 Remove crust from oven. Spread pesto over warm crust. Sprinkle with 1 cup of the mozzarella cheese; top with bell peppers and remaining ¾ cup cheese. Bake 11 to 14 minutes longer or until crust is golden brown and cheese is melted.

1 SERVING: Calories 380; Total Fat 23g (Saturated Fat 8g; Trans Fat 1g); Cholesterol 25mg; Sodium 930mg; Total Carbohydrate 30g (Dietary Fiber 1g); Protein 14g **Exchanges:** 1¹/₂ Starch, ¹/₂ Other Carbohydrate, 1¹/₂ Medium-Fat Meat, 3 Fat **Carbohydrate Choices:** 2

Quick Tip: For a heartier version, add ¹/₄ cup diced smoked ham or cut-up chicken to the pizza toppings.

Caprese Pizza with Crispy Pancetta

PREP TIME: 10 MINUTES • START TO FINISH: 40 MINUTES
8 SERVINGS

1 tablespoon yellow cornmeal

1 1/2 cups Original Bisquick mix

1 1/2 teaspoons Italian seasoning

1/3 cup hot water

1 tablespoon olive oil

1/3 cup refrigerated basil pesto

3 medium tomatoes, cut into
   1/4-inch slices

8 oz fresh mozzarella cheese,
   cut into 1/4-inch slices,
   or 1 1/2 cups shredded
   mozzarella cheese (6 oz)

2 oz diced or sliced pancetta, or
   sliced bacon, crisply cooked,
   crumbled

1/4 cup fresh basil leaves, torn

3 tablespoons balsamic vinegar

1 Heat oven to 350°F. Spray 12-inch pizza pan with cooking spray; sprinkle with cornmeal. In medium bowl, stir Bisquick mix, Italian seasoning, hot water and oil until soft dough forms.

2 On work surface lightly sprinkled with additional Bisquick mix, knead dough until smooth. Press dough in pizza pan. Bake 10 minutes.

3 Spread pesto over warm crust. Arrange tomatoes and mozzarella overlapping in circle on top of pesto. Bake 15 to 20 minutes longer or until crust is golden brown and cheese is melted. Sprinkle with pancetta and basil. Drizzle with balsamic vinegar.

1 SERVING: Calories 300; Total Fat 19g (Saturated Fat 7g; Trans Fat 1g); Cholesterol 25mg; Sodium 700mg; Total Carbohydrate 20g (Dietary Fiber 1g); Protein 13g **Exchanges:** 1 Starch, 1/2 Milk, 1/2 Lean Meat, 2 1/2 Fat **Carbohydrate Choices:** 1

Quick Tip: Sprinkling the pizza pan with cornmeal after spraying adds to the crispness of the crust.

Gluten Free Pizza

PREP TIME: 10 MINUTES   START TO FINISH: 40 MINUTES
6 SERVINGS

CRUST

1$\frac{1}{3}$ cups Bisquick Gluten Free mix

$\frac{1}{2}$ teaspoon Italian seasoning or dried basil leaves

$\frac{1}{2}$ cup water

$\frac{1}{3}$ cup vegetable oil

2 eggs, beaten

SUGGESTED TOPPINGS

1 can (8 oz) pizza sauce

1 cup bite-size pieces favorite meat or vegetables

1$\frac{1}{2}$ cups shredded mozzarella cheese (6 oz)

1 Heat oven to 425°F. Grease 12-inch pizza pan with shortening or cooking spray. In medium bowl, stir Bisquick mix, Italian seasoning, water, oil and eggs with whisk or fork until well combined; spread in pan. Bake 15 minutes (crust will appear cracked).

2 Spread pizza sauce over crust; top with meat and cheese. Bake 10 to 15 minutes longer or until cheese is melted.

1 SERVING: Calories 230; Total Fat 14g (Saturated Fat 2.5g; Trans Fat 0g); Cholesterol 70mg; Sodium 320mg; Total Carbohydrate 23g (Dietary Fiber 0g); Protein 3g **Exchanges:** 1$\frac{1}{2}$ Starch, 2$\frac{1}{2}$ Fat **Carbohydrate Choices:** 1$\frac{1}{2}$

Quick Tip: To save time, purchase cut-up fresh vegetables in the produce section of your supermarket.

Hawaiian Pizza

PREP TIME: 25 MINUTES ⬛ START TO FINISH: 1 HOUR
6 SERVINGS

1 to 2 tablespoons yellow cornmeal

5 oz diced Canadian bacon (1 cup)

2 tablespoons olive oil

²⁄₃ cup chopped green bell pepper

²⁄₃ cup chopped onion

1 can (8 oz) pineapple tidbits in juice, drained

1 can (2¼ oz) sliced ripe olives, drained

1 cup shredded pizza cheese blend (4 oz)

½ cup Original Bisquick mix

⅛ teaspoon pepper

¾ cup milk

⅓ cup sour cream

2 eggs

¾ cup pizza sauce, heated

1 Heat oven to 400°F. Spray 9-inch glass pie plate with cooking spray. Sprinkle inside of pie plate with cornmeal; tap to remove excess. Sprinkle Canadian bacon in bottom of pie plate.

2 In 6-inch nonstick skillet, heat oil over medium heat. Add bell pepper and onion; cook 3 to 5 minutes, stirring occasionally, until tender. Spoon over Canadian bacon. Top with pineapple, olives and cheese blend.

3 In medium bowl, stir Bisquick mix, pepper, milk, sour cream and eggs with whisk or fork until blended. Pour over mixture in pie plate.

4 Bake 25 to 30 minutes or until golden brown and knife inserted in center comes out clean. Let stand 5 minutes before serving. Cut into wedges. Serve with pizza sauce.

1 SERVING: Calories 330; Total Fat 19g (Saturated Fat 8g; Trans Fat 0.5g); Cholesterol 105mg; Sodium 790mg; Total Carbohydrate 22g (Dietary Fiber 2g); Protein 16g **Exchanges:** ½ Fruit, ½ Other Carbohydrate, ½ Low-Fat Milk, ½ Vegetable, 1½ Lean Meat, 2½ Fat **Carbohydrate Choices:** 1½

Quick Tip: Shredded pizza cheese blend is a combination of mozzarella, Cheddar and Monterey Jack cheeses. If you can't find pizza cheese blend, shredded mozzarella is a great substitute.

Stuffed-Crust Pepperoni Pizza

PREP TIME: 20 MINUTES   START TO FINISH: 50 MINUTES
8 SERVINGS

3 cups Original Bisquick mix

²/₃ cup very hot water

2 tablespoons olive or vegetable oil

³/₄ cup diced pepperoni

4 sticks Colby–Monterey Jack cheese (from 10-oz package), cut in half lengthwise

1 can (8 oz) pizza sauce

2 cups shredded Italian cheese blend (8 oz)

1 cup sliced fresh mushrooms (3 oz)

1 small green bell pepper, chopped (¹/₂ cup)

1 can (2¹/₄ oz) sliced ripe olives, drained

1 Move oven rack to lowest position. Heat oven to 450°F. Spray 12-inch pizza pan with cooking spray. In large bowl, stir Bisquick mix, very hot water and oil with fork until soft dough forms; beat vigorously 20 strokes. Let stand 8 minutes.

2 Press dough in bottom and 1 inch over side of pizza pan. Lightly press ¼ cup of the pepperoni along edge of dough. Place string cheese over pepperoni along edge of dough, overlapping if necessary. Fold 1-inch edge of dough over and around cheese and pepperoni; press to seal. Bake 7 minutes.

3 Spread pizza sauce over partially baked crust. Sprinkle with 1 cup of the Italian cheese, remaining ½ cup pepperoni, the mushrooms, bell pepper and olives. Sprinkle with remaining 1 cup Italian cheese.

4 Bake 9 to 12 minutes longer or until crust is golden brown and cheese is melted.

1 SERVING: Calories 430; Total Fat 26g (Saturated Fat 11g; Trans Fat 1.5g); Cholesterol 50mg; Sodium 1310mg; Total Carbohydrate 32g (Dietary Fiber 2g); Protein 16g **Exchanges:** 1¹/₂ Starch, ¹/₂ Other Carbohydrate, 2 High-Fat Meat, 2 Fat **Carbohydrate Choices:** 2

Quick Tip: Cheese sticks may come in slightly different sizes and lengths. If you have a little extra cheese, just overlap the pieces when placing them along the edge of the dough.

Very Veggie Pizza Pie

PREP TIME: 20 MINUTES ▪ **START TO FINISH: 45 MINUTES**
8 SERVINGS

1 package (8 oz) sliced fresh mushrooms (3 cups)

1 small zucchini, sliced (1 cup)

1 medium bell pepper, sliced

1 clove garlic, finely chopped

2 cups Bisquick Heart Smart mix

¼ cup process cheese sauce (room temperature)

¼ cup very hot water

½ cup pizza sauce

¾ cup shredded reduced-fat mozzarella cheese (3 oz)

1 Heat oven to 375°F. Spray cookie sheet with cooking spray. Spray 10-inch skillet with cooking spray; heat over medium-high heat. Add mushrooms, zucchini, bell pepper and garlic; cook about 5 minutes, stirring occasionally, until vegetables are crisp-tender. Set aside.

2 In medium bowl, stir Bisquick mix, cheese sauce and very hot water until soft dough forms. On work surface sprinkled with Bisquick mix, roll dough in Bisquick mix to coat. Knead about 5 times or until smooth.

3 On cookie sheet, roll or pat dough into 14-inch round. Spread pizza sauce over dough to within 3 inches of edge. Top with vegetable mixture. Sprinkle with mozzarella cheese. Fold 3-inch edge of dough up over mixture.

4 Bake 23 to 25 minutes or until crust is golden brown and cheese is bubbly.

1 SERVING: Calories 190; Total Fat 6g (Saturated Fat 2.5g; Trans Fat 0g); Cholesterol 10mg; Sodium 460mg; Total Carbohydrate 25g (Dietary Fiber 1g); Protein 7g **Exchanges:** 1½ Starch, 1 Vegetable, 1 Fat Carbohydrate Choices: 1½

Turkey Gyro Pizza

PREP TIME: 20 MINUTES • **START TO FINISH: 45 MINUTES**
6 SERVINGS

2 cups Original Bisquick mix

$\frac{1}{4}$ **teaspoon dried oregano leaves**

$\frac{1}{2}$ **cup cold water**

$\frac{1}{4}$ **lb sliced cooked turkey breast (from deli), cut into strips**

1 can (2$\frac{1}{4}$ oz) sliced ripe olives, drained

$\frac{1}{2}$ **cup crumbled feta cheese (2 oz)**

1$\frac{1}{2}$ cups shredded mozzarella cheese (6 oz)

1 small tomato, chopped ($\frac{1}{2}$ cup)

$\frac{1}{2}$ **cup chopped cucumber**

1 Heat oven to 425°F. In medium bowl, stir Bisquick mix, oregano and cold water; beat vigorously 20 strokes until soft dough forms.

2 Using fingers dipped in Bisquick mix, press dough in ungreased 12-inch pizza pan; pinch edge to form $\frac{1}{2}$-inch rim. Bake about 15 minutes or until golden brown.

3 Remove partially baked crust from oven. Top with turkey and olives; sprinkle with feta and mozzarella cheeses. Bake about 10 minutes longer or until cheese is melted. Sprinkle with tomato and cucumber.

1 SERVING: Calories 310; Total Fat 15g (Saturated Fat 7g; Trans Fat 1g); Cholesterol 40mg; Sodium 920mg; Total Carbohydrate 27g (Dietary Fiber 1g); Protein 17g **Exchanges:** 1$\frac{1}{2}$ Starch, $\frac{1}{2}$ Other Carbohydrate, 1$\frac{1}{2}$ Lean Meat, 2 Fat **Carbohydrate Choices:** 2

Quick Tip: Oregano and mint are both common herbs used in Greek and Mediterranean cuisine. If you prefer, use mint leaves in place of the oregano here.

CHAPTER 3

Effortless
Breads

Raspberry–White Chocolate Muffins

PREP TIME: 10 MINUTES START TO FINISH: 35 MINUTES
12 MUFFINS

2 cups Original Bisquick mix

¹/₂ cup white vanilla baking chips

¹/₃ cup sugar

²/₃ cup milk

2 tablespoons vegetable oil

1 egg

1 cup raspberries

1 Heat oven to 400°F. Grease bottoms only of 12 regular-size muffin cups with shortening or cooking spray, or place paper baking cup in each muffin cup.

2 In large bowl, stir all ingredients except raspberries just until moistened. Fold in raspberries. Divide batter evenly among muffin cups.

3 Bake 15 to 18 minutes or until golden brown. Cool 5 minutes. Remove from pan to cooling rack. Serve warm.

1 MUFFIN: Calories 190; Total Fat 8g (Saturated Fat 3.5g; Trans Fat 0g); Cholesterol 20mg; Sodium 310mg; Total Carbohydrate 26g (Dietary Fiber 0g); Protein 3g **Exchanges:** 1 Starch, ¹/₂ Other Carbohydrate, 1¹/₂ Fat **Carbohydrate Choices:** 2

Quick Tip: For a sweet finish, dip muffin tops into melted butter and then into coarse sugar crystals or granulated sugar. Or drizzle tops of muffins with melted white vanilla baking chips.

Orange-Almond Streusel Muffins

PREP TIME: 15 MINUTES ▪ START TO FINISH: 30 MINUTES
12 MUFFINS

STREUSEL TOPPING

1 tablespoon Original Bisquick mix

2 tablespoons packed brown sugar

2 tablespoons sliced almonds

1 tablespoon butter or margarine

MUFFINS

⅓ cup packed brown sugar

1 teaspoon grated orange peel

½ cup orange juice

¼ cup vegetable oil

½ teaspoon almond extract

1 egg

2 cups Original Bisquick mix

¼ cup sliced almonds

1 Heat oven to 400°F. Place paper baking cup in each of 12 regular-size muffin cups, or grease bottoms only of muffin cups with shortening.

2 In medium bowl, mix all streusel topping ingredients except butter. Using fork, cut in butter until mixture looks like coarse crumbs; set aside.

3 In large bowl, mix all muffin ingredients except Bisquick mix and ¼ cup almonds. Stir in 2 cups Bisquick mix just until moistened. Stir in ¼ cup almonds. Divide batter evenly among muffin cups. Sprinkle with topping.

4 Bake 13 to 15 minutes or until golden brown. Immediately remove from pan to cooling rack. Serve warm.

1 MUFFIN: Calories 200; Total Fat 11g (Saturated Fat 2.5g; Trans Fat 0.5g); Cholesterol 20mg; Sodium 270mg; Total Carbohydrate 23g (Dietary Fiber 0g); Protein 3g **Exchanges:** 1 Starch, ½ Other Carbohydrate, 2 Fat **Carbohydrate Choices:** 1½

Quick Tip: Serve these muffins warm with honey butter or cream cheese. Add fresh fruit and hot tea for a light breakfast, brunch or snack.

Maple Bacon and Cheddar Muffins

PREP TIME: 20 MINUTES   START TO FINISH: 40 MINUTES
12 MUFFINS

8 oz maple-smoked bacon, cut into 1-inch pieces

1 egg

³⁄₄ cup milk

2 tablespoons butter or margarine, melted

2 cups Original Bisquick mix

³⁄₄ cup shredded Cheddar cheese (3 oz)

¹⁄₄ teaspoon chili powder

1 Heat oven to 400°F. Place paper baking cup in each of 12 regular-size muffin cups; spray paper cups with cooking spray. In 10-inch skillet, cook bacon over medium-high heat, stirring frequently, until crisp. Remove bacon from skillet; drain on paper towel.

2 Meanwhile, in medium bowl, beat egg slightly. Stir in remaining ingredients and bacon just until moistened. Divide batter evenly among muffin cups.

3 Bake 16 to 19 minutes or until golden brown. Immediately remove from pan to cooling rack. Serve warm.

1 MUFFIN: Calories 170; Total Fat 10g (Saturated Fat 4.5g; Trans Fat 0.5g); Cholesterol 35mg; Sodium 470mg; Total Carbohydrate 13g (Dietary Fiber 0g); Protein 6g **Exchanges:** 1 Starch, ¹⁄₂ High-Fat Meat, 1 Fat **Carbohydrate Choices:** 1

Quick Tip: Jazz up these breakfast muffins by substituting Cheddar–Monterey Jack cheese blend with jalapeño peppers for the plain Cheddar cheese. You can find this shredded cheese blend in the dairy section of your supermarket.

Cream Cheese Drop Danish

PREP TIME: 10 MINUTES ◾ START TO FINISH: 20 MINUTES
12 SWEET ROLLS

CREAM CHEESE FILLING

1 package (3 oz) cream cheese, softened

1 tablespoon granulated sugar

1 tablespoon milk

SWEET DOUGH

2 cups Original Bisquick mix

2 tablespoons granulated sugar

¼ cup butter or margarine, softened

⅔ cup milk

VANILLA GLAZE

¾ cup powdered sugar

1 tablespoon warm water

¼ teaspoon vanilla

1 Heat oven to 450°F. Lightly grease cookie sheet with shortening or cooking spray. In small bowl, mix filling ingredients until smooth; set aside.

2 In medium bowl, stir Bisquick mix, 2 tablespoons granulated sugar and the butter until mixture looks like coarse crumbs. Stir in ⅔ cup milk until dough forms; beat with spoon 15 strokes.

3 On cookie sheet, drop dough by rounded tablespoonfuls about 2 inches apart. Make a shallow well in center of each with back of spoon; fill each with about 1 teaspoon filling.

4 Bake 8 to 10 minutes or until golden brown. Meanwhile, in small bowl, mix glaze ingredients until smooth and thin enough to drizzle. Drizzle glaze over warm rolls. Store covered in refrigerator.

1 SWEET ROLL: Calories 190; Total Fat 9g (Saturated Fat 5g; Trans Fat 1g); Cholesterol 20mg; Sodium 300mg; Total Carbohydrate 24g (Dietary Fiber 0g); Protein 3g **Exchanges:** ½ Starch, 1 Other Carbohydrate, 2 Fat **Carbohydrate Choices:** 1½

Quick Tip: Hosting a brunch buffet? You may like to make mini-size drop Danish. Bake just one mini Danish first until you know you have the right bake time for your new mini adventure.

Praline Meltaway Biscuits

PREP TIME: 15 MINUTES ■ START TO FINISH: 30 MINUTES
12 BISCUITS

⅓ cup butter or
   margarine, melted

⅓ cup packed brown sugar

⅓ cup chopped pecans

2¼ cups Original Bisquick mix

2 tablespoons granulated sugar

⅔ cup milk or half-and-half

1 Heat oven to 425°F. Spray bottoms and sides of 12 regular-size muffin cups with cooking spray. In small bowl, stir together butter, brown sugar and pecans. Divide sugar mixture evenly among muffin cups.

2 In medium bowl, stir Bisquick mix, granulated sugar and milk until soft dough forms. Drop spoonful of dough into each muffin cup.

3 Bake 11 to 13 minutes or until golden brown. Turn pan upside down onto cookie sheet. Leave pan over biscuits a few minutes to allow brown sugar mixture to drizzle over biscuits. Remove pan; replace topping from pan onto biscuits. Cool slightly before serving. Serve warm.

1 BISCUIT: Calories 200; Total Fat 10g (Saturated Fat 4.5g, Trans Fat 1g); Cholesterol 15mg; Sodium 330mg; Total Carbohydrate 24g (Dietary Fiber 1g); Protein 2g **Exchanges:** 1 Starch, ½ Other Carbohydrate, 2 Fat **Carbohydrate Choices:** 1½

Quick Tip: You can buy pecans already chopped, or chop them yourself using a chef's knife or food processor (when chopped in a food processor, there will be more very tiny pieces). Store them, tightly wrapped, in the freezer.

Gluten Free Cheese Garlic Biscuits

PREP TIME: 5 MINUTES   START TO FINISH: 15 MINUTES
10 BISCUITS

BISCUITS

2 cups Bisquick Gluten Free mix

¼ teaspoon garlic powder

¼ cup cold butter or margarine

⅔ cup milk

½ cup shredded Cheddar cheese (2 oz)

3 eggs

GARLIC-BUTTER TOPPING

¼ cup butter or margarine, melted

¼ teaspoon garlic powder

1 Heat oven to 425°F. In medium bowl, mix Bisquick mix and ¼ teaspoon garlic powder. Using pastry blender (or pulling 2 table knives through mixture in opposite directions), cut in ¼ cup butter until mixture looks like coarse crumbs. Stir in milk, cheese and eggs until soft dough forms.

2 Drop rounded tablespoonfuls, about 3 inches apart, onto ungreased cookie sheet.

3 Bake 8 to 10 minutes or until light golden brown. In small bowl, mix ¼ cup melted butter and ¼ teaspoon garlic powder; brush over warm biscuits before removing from cookie sheet. Serve warm.

1 BISCUIT: Calories 230; Total Fat 13g (Saturated Fat 8g; Trans Fat 0g); Cholesterol 95mg; Sodium 400mg; Total Carbohydrate 22g (Dietary Fiber 0g); Protein 5g **Exchanges:** 1½ Starch, 2½ Fat **Carbohydrate Choices:** 1½

Quick Tip: Serve these quick biscuits with fresh fruit for a delicious light breakfast.

Gluten Free Biscuits

PREP TIME: 10 MINUTES   START TO FINISH: 30 MINUTES
10 BISCUITS

2 cups Bisquick Gluten Free mix

$\frac{1}{3}$ cup shortening

$\frac{2}{3}$ cup milk

3 eggs

1 Heat oven to 400°F. Place Bisquick mix in large bowl. Using pastry blender (or pulling 2 table knives through ingredients in opposite directions), cut in shortening until mixture looks like coarse crumbs. Stir in remaining ingredients until soft dough forms.

2 Drop dough in rounded tablespoonfuls, 3 inches apart, onto ungreased cookie sheet.

3 Bake 13 to 16 minutes or until golden brown.

1 BISCUIT: Calories 180; Total Fat 9g (Saturated Fat 2.5g; Trans Fat 1g); Cholesterol 65mg; Sodium 300mg; Total Carbohydrate 21g (Dietary Fiber 0g); Protein 3g **Exchanges:** 1$\frac{1}{2}$ Starch, 1$\frac{1}{2}$ Fat **Carbohydrate Choices:** 1$\frac{1}{2}$

Quick Tip: Top warm biscuits with your favorite jelly, jam or honey.

Chocolate Chip Scones

PREP TIME: 10 MINUTES   START TO FINISH: 25 MINUTES
8 SCONES

2 cups Original Bisquick mix

**¹⁄₂ cup semisweet
chocolate chips**

¹⁄₃ cup whipping cream

3 tablespoons sugar

1 teaspoon vanilla

1 egg

Additional whipping cream

Additional sugar

1 Heat oven to 425°F. Spray cookie sheet with cooking spray or grease with shortening. In medium bowl, stir Bisquick mix, chocolate chips, ¹⁄₃ cup whipping cream, 3 tablespoons sugar, the vanilla and egg until soft dough forms.

2 On cookie sheet, pat into 8-inch round (if dough is sticky, dip fingers in Bisquick mix). Brush round with additional whipping cream; sprinkle with additional sugar. Cut into 8 wedges, but do not separate.

3 Bake about 12 minutes or until golden brown. Carefully separate scones. Serve warm.

1 SCONE: Calories 260; Total Fat 12g (Saturated Fat 6g; Trans Fat 1.5g); Cholesterol 45mg; Sodium 380mg; Total Carbohydrate 33g (Dietary Fiber 1g); Protein 3g **Exchanges:** 1 Starch, 1 Other Carbohydrate, 2¹⁄₂ Fat **Carbohydrate Choices:** 2

Quick Tip: Make it even easier by making drop scones. Heat oven to 400°F. Drop dough into 8 mounds onto cookie sheet; pat to slightly flatten. Bake 10 to 12 minutes or until golden brown.

Rosemary-Lemon Cream Scones

PREP TIME: 25 MINUTES START TO FINISH: 50 MINUTES
8 SCONES

SCONES

2 ½ cups Original Bisquick mix

⅓ cup granulated sugar

2 tablespoons cold butter

1 egg, beaten

1 container (6 oz) lemon burst low-fat yogurt

¼ cup heavy whipping cream

1 tablespoon grated lemon peel

1 tablespoon finely chopped fresh rosemary leaves

1 tablespoon heavy whipping cream

1 tablespoon granulated sugar

LEMON DRIZZLE

½ cup powdered sugar

1 tablespoon lemon juice

1 Heat oven to 400°F. Generously spray cookie sheet with cooking spray. In large bowl, mix Bisquick mix and ⅓ cup granulated sugar. Using pastry blender (or pulling 2 table knives through ingredients in opposite directions), cut in butter until mixture looks like coarse crumbs.

2 In small bowl, mix egg, yogurt and ¼ cup whipping cream. Stir into crumb mixture just until combined. Stir in lemon peel and rosemary. Place dough on cookie sheet.

3 With greased hands, pat dough into 8-inch round. Brush dough with 1 tablespoon whipping cream; sprinkle with 1 tablespoon granulated sugar. With sharp knife dipped in additional Bisquick mix, cut into 8 wedges, but do not separate into wedges.

4 Bake 15 to 20 minutes or until light golden brown. Carefully cut into wedges; immediately remove from cookie sheet to cooling rack. Cool 5 minutes. Meanwhile, in small bowl, mix powdered sugar and lemon juice. Drizzle over scones. Serve warm.

1 SCONE: Calories 310; Total Fat 11g (Saturated Fat 5g; Trans Fat 1.5g); Cholesterol 45mg; Sodium 500mg; Total Carbohydrate 47g (Dietary Fiber 1g); Protein 4g **Exchanges:** 1 ½ Starch, 1 ½ Other Carbohydrate, 2 Fat **Carbohydrate Choices:** 3

BETTER WITH BISQUICK

Contest Winner:

Tammy Love • Dallas, NC
This recipe won honorable mention in our Better with Bisquick Contest.

I love to create new recipes. The combination of rosemary and lemon is one of my favorites. And, I love scones! So, my inspiration to create this recipe was from my love of both of these.

Blueberries 'n Orange Bread

PREP TIME: 15 MINUTES   START TO FINISH: 2 HOURS 10 MINUTES
1 LOAF (18 SLICES)

BREAD

3 cups Original Bisquick mix

1/2 cup granulated sugar

**1 tablespoon grated
    orange peel**

1/2 cup milk

3 tablespoons vegetable oil

2 eggs

**1 cup fresh or frozen (rinsed
    and drained) blueberries**

ORANGE GLAZE

1/2 cup powdered sugar

3 to 4 teaspoons orange juice

**Additional grated orange peel,
    If desired**

1 Heat oven to 350°F. Grease bottom only of 9×5-inch loaf pan with shortening or cooking spray. In large bowl, stir all bread ingredients except blueberries until blended. Fold in blueberries. Pour into pan.

2 Bake 50 to 60 minutes or until toothpick inserted in center comes out clean. Cool 10 minutes. Loosen loaf from sides of pan; remove from pan to cooling rack. Cool completely, about 45 minutes.

3 In small bowl, mix powdered sugar and orange juice until smooth and thin enough to drizzle. Drizzle glaze over bread; sprinkle with additional orange peel.

1 SLICE: Calories 150; Total Fat 6g (Saturated Fat 1.5g; Trans Fat 1g); Cholesterol 25mg; Sodium 250mg; Total Carbohydrate 24g (Dietary Fiber 0g); Protein 2g **Exchanges:** 1 Starch, 1/2 Other Carbohydrate, 1 Fat **Carbohydrate Choices:** 1 1/2

Quick Tip: Try other fruit combinations, such as lemon-raspberry or orange-cranberry. Substitute lemon peel and juice for the orange peel and juice, and fresh or frozen raspberries or cranberries for the blueberries.

Sour Cream–Cranberry Bread

PREP TIME: 20 MINUTES   START TO FINISH: 3 HOURS 30 MINUTES
1 LOAF (24 SLICES)

BREAD

2 $\frac{1}{3}$ cups Bisquick Heart
    Smart mix

$\frac{3}{4}$ cup granulated sugar

2 tablespoons grated
    orange peel

$\frac{1}{2}$ cup reduced-fat sour cream

$\frac{1}{4}$ cup vegetable oil

$\frac{1}{4}$ cup fat-free (skim) milk

5 egg whites or $\frac{3}{4}$ cup fat-free
    egg product

$\frac{3}{4}$ cup fresh or frozen
    cranberries, chopped

GLAZE

$\frac{1}{2}$ cup powdered sugar

2 to 3 teaspoons orange juice

1 Heat oven to 375°F. Generously grease bottom of 9×5-inch loaf pan with shortening or cooking spray. In medium bowl, stir all bread ingredients except cranberries until moistened. Stir in cranberries. Pour into pan.

2 Bake 50 to 55 minutes or until toothpick inserted in center comes out clean and top crust is deep golden brown. Cool 15 minutes. Loosen sides of loaf from pan; remove from pan to cooling rack. Cool completely before slicing, about 2 hours. Wrap tightly and store at room temperature up to 4 days, or refrigerate up to 10 days.

3 Before serving, in small bowl, stir powdered sugar and orange juice until smooth and thin enough to drizzle. Drizzle over bread.

1 SLICE: Calories 110; Total Fat 3.5g (Saturated Fat 0.5g; Trans Fat 0g); Cholesterol 0mg; Sodium 115mg; Total Carbohydrate 18g (Dietary Fiber 0g); Protein 2g **Exchanges:** 1 Starch, $\frac{1}{2}$ Fat **Carbohydrate Choices:** 1

Quick Tip: Plan on using two oranges to get the 2 tablespoons grated orange peel called for here. Be sure to grate only the orange part of the skin. The white part or pith is very bitter.

Rosemary and Garlic
Mini Focaccias

PREP TIME: 15 MINUTES   START TO FINISH: 25 MINUTES
24 MINI FOCACCIAS

2 ¼ **cups Original Bisquick mix**

²⁄₃ **cup milk**

2 teaspoons olive or
vegetable oil

½ **teaspoon dried rosemary**
leaves, crumbled

½ **teaspoon garlic powder**

1 Heat oven to 450°F. In medium bowl, stir Bisquick mix and milk until soft dough forms; beat 30 seconds. If dough is too sticky, gradually mix in enough additional Bisquick mix (up to ¼ cup) to make dough easy to handle.

2 On work surface generously dusted with Bisquick mix, gently roll dough in Bisquick mix to coat. Shape into a ball; knead 10 times.

3 Roll out dough until ¼ inch thick. Cut with 2-inch round cutter dipped in Bisquick mix. Place about 2 inches apart on ungreased cookie sheet. Brush with oil; sprinkle with rosemary and garlic powder.

4 Bake 8 to 10 minutes or until golden brown. Serve warm.

1 MINI FOCACCIA: Calories 50; Total Fat 2g (Saturated Fat 0.5g; Trans Fat 0g); Cholesterol 0mg; Sodium 150mg; Total Carbohydrate 8g (Dietary Fiber 0g); Protein 1g **Exchanges:** ½ Starch, ½ Fat **Carbohydrate Choices:** ½

Quick Tip: Reducing the oven temperature to 400°F and placing the cookie sheet on the center oven rack will help the biscuits brown evenly. Serve these miniature focaccia biscuits with any Italian meal.

Green Chile Corn Fritters

PREP TIME: 50 MINUTES   START TO FINISH: 50 MINUTES
4 DOZEN FRITTERS

Vegetable oil for deep frying

4 cups Original Bisquick mix

1 cup cold water

2 eggs

2 cans (15.25 oz each) whole
   kernel corn, drained

2 cans (4.5 oz each) chopped
   green chiles, well drained

Chunky-style salsa, if desired

1 In 3-quart saucepan, heat oil (2 to 3 inches) over medium-high heat until deep-fry thermometer inserted in oil reads 375°F. In large bowl, stir Bisquick mix, cold water and eggs with spoon until smooth. Stir in corn and chiles.

2 Drop batter by small teaspoonfuls into hot oil. Turn and fry until evenly golden brown. Drain on paper towels. Serve with salsa.

1 FRITTER: Calories 100; Total Fat 6g (Saturated Fat 1g; Trans Fat 0g); Cholesterol 10mg; Sodium 260mg; Total Carbohydrate 10g (Dietary Fiber 0g); Protein 1g **Exchanges:** ½ Starch, 1 Fat **Carbohydrate Choices:** ½

Quick Tip: Keep fritters crispy by placing them in an uncovered pan in a 300°F oven.

Sweet Cinnamon Churros

PREP TIME: 35 MINUTES • START TO FINISH: 35 MINUTES
30 CHURROS

Vegetable oil for deep frying

4 tablespoons sugar

2 teaspoons ground cinnamon

3 ¼ cups Original Bisquick mix

1 cup hot water

1 In 3-quart saucepan, heat oil (2 to 3 inches) over medium-high heat until deep-fry thermometer inserted in oil reads 375°F.

2 In small bowl, mix 3 tablespoons of the sugar and the cinnamon; set aside. In medium bowl, stir Bisquick mix, hot water and remaining 1 tablespoon sugar with spatula until dough forms.

3 Spoon dough into pastry bag fitted with ¼-inch star tip. Pipe 5-inch strips of dough into hot oil. If necessary, cut dough with knife or scissors between each churro. Cook 2 to 3 minutes, turning frequently, until golden brown. Carefully remove from oil; drain on paper towels.

4 Immediately sprinkle churros generously with sugar-cinnamon mixture. Serve warm.

1 CHURRO: Calories 150; Total Fat 12g (Saturated Fat 2g; Trans Fat 0g); Cholesterol 0mg; Sodium 160mg; Total Carbohydrate 10g (Dietary Fiber 0g); Protein 1g **Exchanges:** ½ Starch, 2½ Fat **Carbohydrate Choices:** ½

Quick Tip: For a chocolate-covered delight, dip one end of each cooled churro into melted chocolate candy coating, and place on waxed paper until set.

Triple-Cheese Flatbread

PREP TIME: 10 MINUTES **START TO FINISH: 35 MINUTES**
16 SERVINGS

2 cups Original Bisquick mix

$\frac{1}{2}$ cup hot water

2 tablespoons butter or margarine, melted

$\frac{1}{4}$ cup shredded Cheddar cheese (1 oz)

$\frac{1}{4}$ cup shredded Monterey Jack cheese (1 oz)

$\frac{1}{4}$ cup grated Parmesan cheese

$\frac{1}{2}$ teaspoon garlic powder

$\frac{1}{2}$ teaspoon Italian seasoning, if desired

1 Heat oven to 450°F. In medium bowl, stir Bisquick mix and water until stiff dough forms. Let stand 10 minutes.

2 On work surface sprinkled with Bisquick mix, gently roll dough in Bisquick mix to coat. Shape into a ball; knead 60 times.

3 On ungreased cookie sheet, pat or roll dough into 12-inch square. Brush butter over dough. In small bowl, mix remaining ingredients; sprinkle over dough.

4 Bake 10 to 12 minutes or until edges are golden brown. Break into pieces and serve warm.

1 SERVING: Calories 90; Total Fat 5g (Saturated Fat 2.5g; Trans Fat 0.5g); Cholesterol 10mg; Sodium 240mg; Total Carbohydrate 10g (Dietary Fiber 0g); Protein 3g **Exchanges:** $\frac{1}{2}$ Starch, 1 Fat **Carbohydrate Choices:** $\frac{1}{2}$

Quick Tip: To make dough easier to pat onto the cookie sheet, dip your fingers into Bisquick mix.

Mixed Fruit and Yogurt Coffee Cake

PREP TIME: 10 MINUTES • START TO FINISH: 1 HOUR 10 MINUTES

8 SERVINGS

1 package (7 oz) mixed dried fruit, coarsely chopped

¹⁄₂ cup orange juice

1¹⁄₂ cups Original Bisquick mix

¹⁄₂ cup sugar

¹⁄₃ cup plain fat-free yogurt

2 tablespoons butter or margarine, melted

1 teaspoon vanilla

1 egg

1 Heat oven to 350°F. Grease bottom and side of 9-inch round cake pan with shortening; lightly flour. In 1-quart saucepan, heat fruit and orange juice to boiling over medium heat. Reduce heat; simmer about 3 minutes, stirring occasionally, until thickened and fruit is soft. Set aside.

2 In medium bowl, stir remaining ingredients until mixed; pour into pan. Top with fruit mixture.

3 Bake 30 to 40 minutes or until golden brown and toothpick inserted in center comes out clean. Cool 20 minutes before serving.

1 SERVING: Calories 260; Total Fat 6g (Saturated Fat 3g; Trans Fat 1g); Cholesterol 35mg; Sodium 320mg; Total Carbohydrate 46g (Dietary Fiber 2g); Protein 4g **Exchanges:** 1 Starch, ¹⁄₂ Fruit, 1¹⁄₂ Other Carbohydrate, 1 Fat **Carbohydrate Choices:** 3

Quick Tip: If necessary, cover the coffee cake with foil halfway through baking to keep the fruit from overbrowning.

Apples 'n Brown Sugar Coffee Cake

PREP TIME: 15 MINUTES   START TO FINISH: 1 HOUR
8 SERVINGS

STREUSEL TOPPING

²/₃ **cup Original Bisquick mix**

²/₃ **cup packed brown sugar**

1 teaspoon ground cinnamon

¹/₂ **teaspoon ground nutmeg**

¹/₄ **cup cold butter or margarine**

COFFEE CAKE

2 cups Original Bisquick mix

3 tablespoons granulated sugar

²/₃ **cup milk or water**

1 egg

2 medium cooking apples, peeled, thinly sliced (2 cups)

2 tablespoons chopped nuts

GLAZE

¹/₂ **cup powdered sugar**

2 to 3 teaspoons milk

1 Heat oven to 400°F. Spray 9-inch square pan with cooking spray. In small bowl, mix ⅔ cup Bisquick mix, the brown sugar, cinnamon and nutmeg. Using pastry blender (or pulling 2 knives through ingredients in opposite directions), cut in butter until mixture looks like coarse crumbs; set aside.

2 In medium bowl, stir together 2 cups Bisquick mix, granulated sugar, ⅔ cup milk and the egg; beat vigorously 30 seconds. Spread half of the batter in pan. Arrange apple slices on batter; sprinkle with half of the streusel topping. Spread with remaining batter; sprinkle with remaining topping. Sprinkle with nuts.

3 Bake about 25 minutes or until toothpick inserted in center comes out clean. Cool 20 minutes. In small bowl, stir glaze ingredients until thin enough to drizzle. Drizzle over warm coffee cake.

1 SERVING: Calories 380; Total Fat 13g (Saturated Fat 6g; Trans Fat 2g); Cholesterol 45mg; Sodium 550mg; Total Carbohydrate 62g (Dietary Fiber 2g); Protein 5g **Exchanges:** 1¹/₂ Starch, 2¹/₂ Other Carbohydrate, 2¹/₂ Fat **Carbohydrate Choices:** 4

Quick Tip: This coffee cake is a great make-ahead treat, to serve when unexpected guests drop by. Wrap it tightly, and freeze for up to 2 months. Thaw and heat in microwave or oven to serve warm.

Gluten Free Cinnamon Streusel Coffee Cake

PREP TIME: 10 MINUTES   START TO FINISH: 40 MINUTES
6 SERVINGS

STREUSEL TOPPING

1/3 **cup Bisquick Gluten Free mix**

1/2 **cup packed brown sugar**

3/4 **teaspoon ground cinnamon**

1/4 **cup cold butter or margarine**

COFFEE CAKE

1 3/4 **cups Bisquick Gluten Free mix**

3 **tablespoons granulated sugar**

2/3 **cup milk or water**

1 1/2 **teaspoons vanilla**

3 **eggs**

1 Heat oven to 350°F. Spray 9-inch round or square pan with cooking spray. In small bowl, mix 1/3 cup Bisquick mix, the brown sugar and cinnamon. Using pastry blender (or pulling 2 knives through ingredients in opposite directions), cut in butter until mixture looks like coarse crumbs; set aside.

2 In medium bowl, stir coffee cake ingredients with whisk or fork until blended. Spread in pan; sprinkle with topping.

3 Bake 25 to 30 minutes or until golden brown. Store tightly covered.

1 SERVING: Calories 380; Total Fat 11g (Saturated Fat 6g; Trans Fat 0g); Cholesterol 130mg; Sodium 570mg; Total Carbohydrate 62g (Dietary Fiber 1g); Protein 6g **Exchanges:** 2 Starch, 2 Other Carbohydrate, 2 Fat **Carbohydrate Choices:** 4

CHAPTER 4

Main-Dish
Mainstays

Buffalo Chicken Pie

PREP TIME: 15 MINUTES • START TO FINISH: 45 MINUTES
6 SERVINGS

2 cups cooked chicken strips

¹/₂ cup Buffalo wing sauce

1 cup shredded Cheddar cheese (4 oz)

¹/₂ cup crumbled blue cheese (2 oz)

1 cup chopped celery (about 2¹/₂ stalks)

1 cup Original Bisquick mix

¹/₂ cup cornmeal

¹/₂ cup milk

1 egg

²/₃ cup blue cheese dressing

1 Heat oven to 400°F. In large bowl, toss chicken and Buffalo wing sauce until well coated. Stir in cheeses and celery. Pour into ungreased 9-inch glass pie plate.

2 In medium bowl, mix Bisquick mix, cornmeal, milk and egg. Pour over chicken mixture; spread to cover.

3 Bake 25 to 30 minutes or until topping is golden brown. Cut into wedges; drizzle with blue cheese dressing.

1 SERVING: Calories 510; Total Fat 30g (Saturated Fat 10g; Trans Fat 1g); Cholesterol 110mg; Sodium 1180mg; Total Carbohydrate 36g (Dietary Fiber 1g); Protein 25g **Exchanges:** 2 Starch, ¹/₂ Other Carbohydrate, 2¹/₂ Lean Meat, 4 Fat **Carbohydrate Choices:** 2¹/₂

Quick Tip: For extra-speedy dinner preparation, look for packages of refrigerated cooked chicken strips to use in this recipe.

BETTER WITH BISQUICK

Contest Winner:

**Jamie Jones •
Madison, GA**

This recipe won 3rd place in our Better with Bisquick Contest.

This recipe came about the Monday after the Super Bowl, when I needed a quick and easy dish for dinner for my busy family. I opened the fridge and had leftovers from the big game party.

Chicken Enchilada Casserole

PREP TIME: 20 MINUTES   START TO FINISH: 55 MINUTES
8 SERVINGS

2 cups diced cooked chicken

1 can (15.5 oz) pinto beans, drained, rinsed

$\frac{1}{2}$ cup chunky-style salsa

3 teaspoons chili powder

$\frac{1}{4}$ teaspoon garlic powder

$\frac{1}{2}$ loaf (16-oz size) prepared cheese product, cut into cubes

1 cup Original Bisquick mix

$\frac{3}{4}$ cup milk

2 tablespoons butter, melted

1 cup shredded lettuce

1 plum (Roma) tomato, diced ($\frac{1}{2}$ cup)

4 medium green onions, sliced ($\frac{1}{4}$ cup)

1 Heat oven to 425°F. Spray 2-quart round casserole or 11×7-inch (2-quart) glass baking dish with cooking spray. In large bowl, mix chicken, beans, salsa, chili powder and garlic powder; stir in cheese. Spoon into baking dish.

2 In small bowl, mix Bisquick mix, milk and butter. Pour and spoon evenly over chicken mixture.

3 Bake 30 to 35 minutes or until crust is golden brown. Top with lettuce, tomato and onions. If desired, serve with guacamole, sour cream and pickled sliced jalapeño chiles.

1 SERVING: Calories 350; Total Fat 16g (Saturated Fat 9g; Trans Fat 1g); Cholesterol 65mg; Sodium 610mg; Total Carbohydrate 28g (Dietary Fiber 6g); Protein 24g **Exchanges:** 1½ Starch, ½ Vegetable, 2½ Medium-Fat Meat, ½ Fat **Carbohydrate Choices:** 2

Quick Tip: Use leftover chicken or rotisserie chicken in this recipe, or look for diced cooked chicken in the refrigerator or freezer case of the grocery store.

BETTER WITH BISQUICK

Contest Winner:

**Denise Maurice •
Baltimore, MD**

This recipe won honorable mention in our Better with Bisquick Contest.

My mom made a lot of different recipes that used Bisquick. This is one of the recipes that she handed down. There were five kids in the family, and my mom ran a ceramics shop out of our home.

Impossibly Easy Mexicali Chicken Pie

PREP TIME: 20 MINUTES • START TO FINISH: 50 MINUTES
6 TO 8 SERVINGS

1 cup chopped or shredded
  cooked chicken

1 cup frozen whole kernel corn

1 can (2¼ oz) sliced ripe
  olives, drained

1 small onion, chopped (¼ cup)

1 tablespoon chopped green
  chiles (from 4.5-oz can)

2 cups shredded Monterey Jack
  cheese (8 oz)

½ cup Original Bisquick mix

1 cup milk

2 eggs

½ teaspoon salt

¼ teaspoon pepper

½ cup sour cream

½ cup guacamole

1 cup chunky-style salsa

1 Heat oven to 400°F. Spray 9-inch glass pie plate or 8-inch square (2-quart) glass baking dish with cooking spray. In large bowl, mix chicken, corn, olives, onion, chiles and cheese. Spoon into pie plate.

2 In medium bowl, stir Bisquick mix, milk, eggs, salt and pepper with whisk until tiny lumps remain. Pour evenly over chicken mixture.

3 Bake 28 to 30 minutes or until knife inserted in center comes out clean. Top with sour cream, guacamole, and salsa.

1 SERVING: Calories 380; Total Fat 23g (Saturated Fat 12g; Trans Fat 1g); Cholesterol 135mg; Sodium 1080mg; Total Carbohydrate 20g (Dietary Fiber 2g); Protein 21g **Exchanges:** ½ Starch, ½ Other Carbohydrate, ½ Vegetable, 2½ Medium-Fat Meat, 2 Fat **Carbohydrate Choices:** 1

Quick Tip: To quickly thaw frozen corn, place in colander or strainer; rinse with warm water until thawed. Drain well.

BETTER WITH BISQUICK

Contest Winner:

**Jackie Colwell •
Oregon City, OR**

This recipe
won honorable
mention in our Better with
Bisquick Contest.

Easy Chicken Pot Pie

PREP TIME: 10 MINUTES · START TO FINISH: 40 MINUTES

6 SERVINGS

1 bag (12 oz) frozen mixed
    vegetables, thawed, drained

1 cup diced cooked chicken

1 can (10 3/4 oz) condensed
    cream of chicken soup

1 cup Original Bisquick mix

1/2 cup milk

1 egg

1 Heat oven to 400°F. In ungreased 1½-quart casserole, mix vegetables, chicken and soup until blended.

2 In medium bowl, stir all remaining ingredients with whisk or fork until blended. Pour over chicken mixture.

3 Bake uncovered about 30 minutes or until crust is golden brown.

1 SERVING: Calories 240; Total Fat 9g (Saturated Fat 3g, Trans Fat 1g); Cholesterol 60mg; Sodium 670mg; Total Carbohydrate 28g (Dietary Fiber 4g); Protein 13g **Exchanges:** 1½ Starch, 1 Vegetable, 1 Lean Meat, 1 Fat **Carbohydrate Choices:** 2

Quick Tip: If you don't have mixed vegetables on hand, use 3 cups of any frozen vegetable combination.

Impossibly Easy Chicken Cordon Bleu Pie

PREP TIME: 15 MINUTES START TO FINISH: 55 MINUTES
6 SERVINGS

1 cup cubed cooked chicken

²/₃ cup cubed cooked ham

1 cup shredded Swiss cheese (4 oz)

¹/₂ cup Original Bisquick mix

¹/₄ teaspoon salt

¹/₈ teaspoon pepper

²/₃ cup milk

¹/₃ cup chicken broth

¹/₄ cup chive-and-onion sour cream potato topper (from 12-oz container)

2 teaspoons Dijon mustard

2 eggs

Additional chive-and-onion sour cream potato topper, if desired

Chopped fresh chives, if desired

1 Heat oven to 400°F. Spray 9-inch glass pie plate with cooking spray. Layer chicken, ham, and cheese in pie plate.

2 In medium bowl, mix remaining ingredients with whisk or fork until blended. Pour over cheese in pie plate.

3 Bake 30 to 35 minutes or until knife inserted in center comes out clean. Let stand 5 minutes before serving. Serve with additional potato topper and chives.

1 SERVING: Calories 240; Total Fat 13g (Saturated Fat 6g; Trans Fat 0.5g); Cholesterol 120mg; Sodium 660mg; Total Carbohydrate 10g (Dietary Fiber 0g); Protein 19g **Exchanges:** ¹/₂ Other Carbohydrate, ¹/₂ Low-Fat Milk, 2 Lean Meat, 1 Fat **Carbohydrate Choices:** ¹/₂

Quick Tip: For a quick way to get cooked chicken, pick up a rotisserie chicken at your supermarket.

Impossibly Easy Buffalo Chicken Pie

PREP TIME: 20 MINUTES   START TO FINISH: 1 HOUR
6 SERVINGS

¼ cup blue cheese dressing

¼ cup red pepper sauce

1 package (3 oz) cream cheese, softened

1¼ cups cubed cooked chicken

½ cup chopped celery

¼ cup sliced green onions (4 medium)

1 cup shredded Swiss cheese (4 oz)

¾ cup Original Bisquick mix

½ teaspoon salt

¼ teaspoon pepper

¾ cup milk

3 eggs

Additional blue cheese dressing, if desired

1 Heat oven to 400°F. Spray 9-inch glass pie plate with cooking spray. In small bowl, mix dressing, pepper sauce and cream cheese until blended. Spread in bottom of pie plate. Top with chicken, celery, green onions and Swiss cheese.

2 In medium bowl, stir remaining ingredients with whisk or fork until blended. Pour into pie plate.

3 Bake 25 to 30 minutes or until top is golden brown and center is set. Let stand 10 minutes before serving. Serve with additional dressing.

1 SERVING: Calories 350; Total Fat 23g (Saturated Fat 9g; Trans Fat 1g); Cholesterol 170mg; Sodium 920mg; Total Carbohydrate 17g (Dietary Fiber 1g); Protein 19g **Exchanges:** ½ Starch, ½ Low-Fat Milk, 2 Lean Meat, 3 Fat **Carbohydrate Choices:** 1

Gluten Free Hearty Chicken Pie

PREP TIME: 15 MINUTES ▪ **START TO FINISH: 45 MINUTES**
6 SERVINGS

CHICKEN MIXTURE

2 tablespoons butter or margarine

1 medium onion, chopped (¹/₂ cup)

1 bag (12 oz) frozen mixed vegetables

1¹/₂ cups cut-up cooked chicken

1³/₄ cups chicken broth

1 teaspoon seasoned salt

¹/₂ teaspoon dried thyme

³/₄ cup milk

3 tablespoons cornstarch

TOPPING

³/₄ cup Bisquick Gluten Free mix

¹/₂ cup milk

1 egg

2 tablespoons butter or margarine, melted

1 tablespoon chopped fresh parsley

1 Heat oven to 350°F. In 3-quart saucepan, melt butter over medium heat. Add onion; cook, stirring frequently, until tender. Stir in vegetables, chicken, broth, salt and thyme; heat to boiling. In small bowl, mix ¾ cup milk and the cornstarch with whisk until smooth; stir into chicken mixture. Heat just to boiling. Pour into ungreased 2-quart casserole.

2 In small bowl, stir all topping ingredients except parsley with whisk or fork until blended. Drop topping mixture by small spoonfuls over chicken mixture. Sprinkle with parsley.

3 Bake uncovered 25 to 30 minutes or until toothpick inserted in center of topping comes out clean.

1 SERVING: Calories 290; Total Fat 13g (Saturated Fat 7g; Trans Fat 0g); Cholesterol 90mg; Sodium 830mg; Total Carbohydrate 28g (Dietary Fiber 3g); Protein 16g **Exchanges:** 1¹/₂ Starch, 1 Vegetable, 1¹/₂ Lean Meat, 1¹/₂ Fat **Carbohydrate Choices:** 2

Light Lemon-Sesame Chicken

PREP TIME: 30 MINUTES • START TO FINISH: 30 MINUTES
4 SERVINGS

CHICKEN

4 boneless skinless chicken breasts (about 1¼ lb)

¼ cup fat-free egg product or 1 egg

2 tablespoons lemon juice

½ cup Bisquick Heart Smart mix

½ teaspoon paprika

2 tablespoons toasted sesame seed*

1 tablespoon canola or vegetable oil

SAUCE

½ cup Progresso chicken broth (from 32-oz carton)

3 tablespoons sugar

2 tablespoons lemon juice

2 teaspoons cornstarch

1 teaspoon grated lemon peel

2 medium green onions, sliced (2 tablespoons)

1 Between pieces of plastic wrap or waxed paper, place each chicken breast smooth side down; gently pound with flat side of meat mallet or rolling pin until about ¼ inch thick.

2 In small bowl, beat egg product and 2 tablespoons lemon juice with fork or whisk until blended. In 1-gallon resealable food-storage plastic bag, place Bisquick mix, paprika and sesame seed. Dip chicken into egg mixture, then place in bag; shake until well coated.

3 In 12-inch nonstick skillet, heat oil over medium-high heat. Cook chicken in oil 6 to 8 minutes, turning once, until no longer pink in center.

4 Meanwhile, in 1-quart saucepan, heat all sauce ingredients except onions over medium heat, stirring occasionally, until thickened and bubbly. Serve sauce over chicken; sprinkle with onions.

1 SERVING: Calories 340; Total Fat 11g (Saturated Fat 2g, Trans Fat 0g); Cholesterol 90mg; Sodium 440mg; Total Carbohydrate 24g (Dietary Fiber 1g); Protein 36g **Exchanges:** ½ Starch, 1 Other Carbohydrate, 4½ Lean Meat **Carbohydrate Choices:** 1½

*Toasted sesame seed is available in the spice section or Asian aisle of the supermarket. Or, to toast regular sesame seed, cook in ungreased heavy skillet over medium-low heat 5 to 7 minutes, stirring frequently until browning begins, then stirring constantly until golden brown.

Salsa Burrito Bake

PREP TIME: 20 MINUTES • START TO FINISH: 50 MINUTES

8 SERVINGS

2 cups Original Bisquick mix

¹⁄₂ cup cold water

1 can (16 oz) refried beans

2 cups cooked rice

¹⁄₂ cup chunky-style salsa

2 cups shredded Cheddar cheese (8 oz)

1 cup chopped tomato

¹⁄₄ cup sliced ripe olives

2 cups shredded lettuce

Additional chunky-style salsa, if desired

Sour cream, if desired

1 Heat oven to 375°F. Spray 13×9-inch pan with cooking spray. In medium bowl, stir Bisquick mix and cold water until soft dough forms. Press evenly in bottom of pan. Spread beans over crust.

2 In small bowl, stir together rice and ½ cup salsa. Spread evenly over beans. Top with cheese.

3 Bake 25 to 30 minutes or until cheese is melted and crust is golden brown. Top with tomatoes, olives and lettuce. Serve with additional salsa and sour cream.

1 SERVING: Calories 350; Total Fat 14g (Saturated Fat 7g; Trans Fat 1.5g); Cholesterol 30mg; Sodium 1100mg; Total Carbohydrate 42g (Dietary Fiber 4g); Protein 13g **Exchanges:** 2¹⁄₂ Starch, ¹⁄₂ Vegetable, 1 Lean Meat, 2 Fat **Carbohydrate Choices:** 3

Quick Tip: If you don't have cooked rice on hand, use instant rice or boil-in-the bag rice to have cooked rice in 10 minutes.

Chile Relleno Casserole

PREP TIME: 25 MINUTES • START TO FINISH: 1 HOUR

8 SERVINGS

1 lb lean (at least 80%) ground beef

1 medium onion, chopped (½ cup)

½ teaspoon chili powder

¼ teaspoon ground cumin

¼ teaspoon salt, if desired

⅛ teaspoon pepper

3 eggs, slightly beaten

1 cup milk

2 cups Original Bisquick mix

2 cups shredded Colby–Monterey Jack cheese blend (8 oz)

2 cans (4 oz each) peeled whole green chiles, drained

Chunky-style salsa, if desired

Thinly sliced green onion, if desired

1 Heat oven to 350F. Spray 12×8-inch or 11×7-inch (2-quart) glass baking dish with cooking spray. In 10-inch skillet, cook beef, onion, chili powder, cumin, salt and pepper over medium-high heat 5 to 7 minutes, stirring occasionally, until beef is thoroughly cooked; drain.

2 In medium bowl, mix eggs, milk and Bisquick mix with whisk or fork until only tiny lumps remain. Pour half of the batter into baking dish. Sprinkle with 1 cup of the cheese. Spoon beef mixture evenly over cheese.

3 Using paring knife, cut lengthwise slit down long edge of each chile; open and arrange flat on beef mixture, overlapping if necessary. Sprinkle with remaining 1 cup cheese. Pour remaining batter on top to cover.

4 Bake uncovered 25 to 35 minutes or until topping is light golden brown. Top with salsa and sprinkle with green onion.

1 SERVING: Calories 380; Total Fat 22g (Saturated Fat 10g; Trans Fat 2g); Cholesterol 145mg; Sodium 700mg; Total Carbohydrate 24g (Dietary Fiber 1g); Protein 22g **Exchanges:** 1½ Starch, 2½ Medium-Fat Meat, 1½ Fat **Carbohydrate Choices:** 1½

BETTER WITH BISQUICK

Contest Winner:

Kathy Davis • Hobbs, NM

This recipe won honorable mention in our Better with Bisquick Contest.

Quick Tip: While this main dish bakes, toss together a crisp tossed salad to serve with your favorite dressing.

Three-Cheese Spinach and Pasta Bake

PREP TIME: 30 MINUTES **START TO FINISH: 1 HOUR 15 MINUTES**
10 SERVINGS

1 package (8 oz) sliced fresh
   mushrooms (about 3 cups)

1/4 cup finely chopped onion

1 package (7 oz) small pasta
   shells, cooked, drained

2 boxes (9 oz each) frozen
   spinach, thawed, squeezed
   to drain

1 cup Original Bisquick mix

1 cup shredded mozzarella
   cheese (4 oz)

1/3 cup grated Parmesan cheese

1 teaspoon salt

1/2 teaspoon pepper

1 3/4 cups milk

1 package (4 oz) crumbled
   tomato-basil feta cheese
   (1 cup)

1 Heat oven to 375°F. Spray 13×9-inch (3-quart) glass baking dish with cooking spray. In 8-inch nonstick skillet, cook mushrooms and onion over medium heat about 5 minutes, stirring frequently, until tender.

2 In large bowl, stir together pasta and spinach. Stir in mushroom mixture. Spread in baking dish.

3 In large bowl, stir remaining ingredients until blended. Pour over spinach mixture.

4 Bake uncovered 35 to 40 minutes or until top is golden brown. Let stand 5 minutes before serving.

1 SERVING: Calories 200; Total Fat 9g (Saturated Fat 5g; Trans Fat 0.5g); Cholesterol 25mg; Sodium 700mg; Total Carbohydrate 20g (Dietary Fiber 2g); Protein 11g **Exchanges:** 1 Starch, 1/2 Low-Fat Milk, 1/2 Vegetable, 1 Fat **Carbohydrate Choices:** 1

Quick Tip: For extra speedy prep, purchase mushrooms already sliced, and frozen chopped onions. Thaw the spinach quickly in the microwave—1 to 2 minutes will do the trick.

Smoky BBQ Cups

PREP TIME: 20 MINUTES • START TO FINISH: 35 MINUTES
12 SERVINGS

1 lb lean (at least 80%) ground beef

¼ cup finely chopped onion

1 cup hickory smoke-flavored barbecue sauce

2¼ cups Original Bisquick mix

1 cup shredded Cheddar cheese (4 oz)

⅔ cup milk

1 Heat oven to 450°F. Spray 12 regular-size muffin cups with cooking spray. In 10-inch nonstick skillet, cook beef and onion over medium-high heat 5 to 7 minutes, stirring occasionally, until thoroughly cooked; drain. Stir in barbecue sauce; cook until mixture just begins to bubble.

2 In medium bowl, stir Bisquick mix, ½ cup of the cheese and the milk until soft dough forms. Spoon about 2 tablespoons dough into each muffin cup. Press dough in bottom and up side of each cup. Spoon 2 tablespoons beef mixture into each cup.

3 Bake 8 to 10 minutes or until top edges of cups are golden brown. Sprinkle each with remaining cheese. Let stand 5 minutes; remove from pan.

1 SERVING: Calories 240; Total Fat 11g (Saturated Fat 4.5g; Trans Fat 1g); Cholesterol 35mg; Sodium 580mg; Total Carbohydrate 25g (Dietary Fiber 0g); Protein 11g **Exchanges:** ½ Starch, 1 Other Carbohydrate, ½ Low-Fat Milk, 1 Lean Meat, 1 Fat **Carbohydrate Choices:** 1½

Quick Tip: For easy, correct Bisquick mix measuring, spoon into dry-ingredient measuring cup, and level with a straight-edged knife or spatula. Do not pack or tap Bisquick mix into cup.

Gluten Free Impossibly Easy Cheeseburger Pie

PREP TIME: 15 MINUTES   START TO FINISH: 45 MINUTES
6 SERVINGS

1 lb lean (at least 80%) ground beef

1 medium onion, chopped (½ cup)

½ teaspoon salt

⅛ teaspoon pepper

1 cup shredded Cheddar cheese (4 oz)

½ cup Bisquick Gluten Free mix

1 cup milk

3 eggs

1 Heat oven to 400°F. Spray 9-inch glass pie plate with cooking spray. In 10-inch skillet, cook beef and onion over medium-high heat, stirring frequently, until beef is thoroughly cooked; drain. Stir in salt and pepper. Spread in pie plate; sprinkle with cheese.

2 In medium bowl, stir Bisquick mix, milk and eggs with whisk or fork until blended. Pour into pie plate.

3 Bake 25 to 30 minutes or until knife inserted in center comes out clean.

1 SERVING: Calories 310; Total Fat 18g (Saturated Fat 9g; Trans Fat 1g); Cholesterol 175mg; Sodium 510mg; Total Carbohydrate 13g (Dietary Fiber 0g); Protein 23g **Exchanges:** 1 Starch, 2½ Medium-Fat Meat, 1 Fat **Carbohydrate Choices:** 1

Quick Tip: Serve with ketchup, barbecue sauce or salsa for an easy punch of flavor.

Impossibly Easy Chili Pie

PREP TIME: 20 MINUTES   START TO FINISH: 1 HOUR

6 SERVINGS

1 lb lean (at least 80%) ground beef

1 can (14.5 oz) diced tomatoes, drained

1 medium onion, chopped (½ cup)

1 envelope (1 oz) chili seasoning mix

1 can (2¼ oz) sliced ripe olives, drained

1 cup shredded Cheddar cheese (4 oz)

½ cup Original Bisquick mix

1 cup milk

2 eggs

Chopped tomato, red onion and jalapeño, if desired

Sour cream, if desired

1 Heat oven to 400°F. Spray 9-inch glass pie plate with cooking spray. In 10-inch skillet, cook beef over medium heat 8 to 10 minutes, stirring occasionally, until browned; drain. Stir in tomatoes, onion and chili seasoning mix. Spread in pie plate. Sprinkle with olives and ½ cup of the cheese.

2 In medium bowl, stir Bisquick mix, milk and eggs with whisk or fork until blended. Pour into pie plate.

3 Bake 30 minutes. Top with remaining ½ cup cheese. Bake 2 to 3 minutes longer or until cheese is melted. Let stand 5 minutes before serving. Serve with chopped vegetables and sour cream.

1 SERVING: Calories 270; Total Fat 11g (Saturated Fat 4g; Trans Fat 0.5g); Cholesterol 50mg; Sodium 810mg; Total Carbohydrate 18g (Dietary Fiber 2g); Protein 24g **Exchanges:** 1 Starch, 1 Vegetable, 3 Medium-Fat Meat, 1 Fat **Carbohydrate Choices:** 1

Quick Tip: For an easy topping, substitute salsa for fresh vegetables.

Italian Artichoke-Bacon Pie

PREP TIME: 15 MINUTES • START TO FINISH: 50 MINUTES
6 SERVINGS

1 cup shredded mozzarella cheese (4 oz)

12 slices bacon, crisply cooked, crumbled (³/₄ cup)

¹/₄ cup chopped sun-dried tomatoes in olive oil, drained

¹/₄ cup creamy Italian dressing

1 jar (6 oz) marinated artichoke hearts, drained, chopped

¹/₂ cup Original Bisquick mix

¹/₄ cup grated Parmesan cheese

¹/₂ teaspoon garlic powder

1 cup milk

2 eggs

1 Heat oven to 400°F. Spray 9-inch glass pie plate with cooking spray. In large bowl, toss mozzarella cheese, bacon, sun-dried tomatoes, dressing and artichokes. Spread mixture in pie plate.

2 In medium bowl, beat remaining ingredients with whisk or fork until blended. Pour over mixture in pie plate.

3 Bake 25 to 30 minutes or until golden brown and knife inserted in center comes out clean. Let stand 5 minutes before serving.

1 SERVING: Calories 280; Total Fat 17g (Saturated Fat 6g; Trans Fat 0.5g); Cholesterol 100mg; Sodium 820mg; Total Carbohydrate 16g (Dietary Fiber 3g); Protein 15g **Exchanges:** 1 Starch, ¹/₂ Vegetable, 1¹/₂ Medium-Fat Meat, 2 Fat **Carbohydrate Choices:** 1

Quick Tip: A terrific convenience product and a real time-saver, packaged precooked bacon is available both in slices and pieces.

Stromboli Squares

PREP TIME: 20 MINUTES • START TO FINISH: 55 MINUTES
9 SERVINGS

³/₄ lb bulk Italian pork sausage

2 cups Original Bisquick mix

1 cup milk

2 eggs

¹/₄ lb thinly sliced pepperoni (about 56 slices)

1 cup shredded mozzarella cheese (4 oz)

1 jar (7 oz) roasted red bell peppers, drained, cut into strips

1 teaspoon water

1 teaspoon poppy seed

Marinara sauce, if desired

1 Heat oven to 375°F. Spray 8-inch square (2-quart) glass baking dish with cooking spray. In 10-inch nonstick skillet, cook sausage over medium heat, stirring occasionally, until no longer pink; set aside.

2 In medium bowl, stir Bisquick mix, milk and 1 of the eggs with whisk or fork until blended. Spread half of the batter in baking dish. Top with sausage, pepperoni, cheese and roasted pepper strips. Pour remaining batter over mixture in dish; spread to cover.

3 In small bowl, beat remaining 1 egg and the water. Carefully brush over batter; sprinkle with poppy seed.

4 Bake 25 to 30 minutes or until golden brown. Let stand 5 minutes before serving. Serve with marinara sauce.

1 SERVING: Calories 340; Total Fat 21g (Saturated Fat 8g; Trans Fat 1.5g); Cholesterol 85mg; Sodium 960mg; Total Carbohydrate 22g (Dietary Fiber 1g); Protein 16g **Exchanges:** 1 Starch, ¹/₂ Low-Fat Milk, 1¹/₂ Lean Meat, 2¹/₂ Fat **Carbohydrate Choices:** 1¹/₂

Quick Tip: You can use ³/₄ cup of chopped red or green pepper in place of the roasted red bell peppers.

Macaroni and Cheese Pie

PREP TIME: 15 MINUTES • START TO FINISH: 1 HOUR 10 MINUTES
6 SERVINGS

3 cups shredded Cheddar
cheese (12 oz)

1 cup cubed cooked ham

1 cup uncooked elbow macaroni
(3½ oz)

2¼ cups milk

2 eggs

½ cup Original Bisquick mix

¼ teaspoon salt

Chopped fresh parsley,
if desired

1 Heat oven to 400°F. Spray 10-inch or 9½-inch glass deep-dish pie plate with cooking spray. In large bowl, mix 2 cups of the cheese, the ham and macaroni. Spread in pie plate.

2 In blender, place milk and eggs. Cover; blend on medium speed until smooth. Add Bisquick mix and salt; blend until smooth. Pour over mixture in pie plate.

3 Bake 35 to 40 minutes or until knife inserted in center comes out clean. Sprinkle with remaining 1 cup cheese. Bake 1 to 2 minutes longer or until cheese is melted. Let stand 10 minutes before serving. Sprinkle with parsley.

1 SERVING: Calories 470; Total Fat 26g (Saturated Fat 15g; Trans Fat 1g); Cholesterol 150mg; Sodium 1050mg; Total Carbohydrate 30g (Dietary Fiber 1g); Protein 28g **Exchanges:** ½ Other Carbohydrate, 2 Low-Fat Milk, 1½ Lean Meat, 2½ Fat **Carbohydrate Choices:** 2

Impossibly Easy BLT Pie

PREP TIME: 20 MINUTES   START TO FINISH: 55 MINUTES
6 SERVINGS

12 slices bacon

1 cup shredded Swiss cheese (4 oz)

$\frac{1}{2}$ cup Original Bisquick mix

$\frac{1}{3}$ cup mayonnaise or salad dressing

$\frac{3}{4}$ cup milk

$\frac{1}{8}$ teaspoon pepper

2 eggs

2 tablespoons mayonnaise or salad dressing

1 cup shredded lettuce

6 thin slices tomato

1 Heat oven to 400°F. Spray 9-inch glass pie plate with cooking spray. Line microwavable plate with microwavable paper towel. Place 6 slices of the bacon on paper towel; cover with another paper towel. Microwave on High 4 to 6 minutes or until crisp. Repeat with remaining 6 slices bacon. Crumble bacon. Layer bacon and cheese in pie plate.

2 In medium bowl, beat Bisquick mix, $\frac{1}{3}$ cup mayonnaise, the milk, pepper and eggs with whisk or fork until blended. Pour into pie plate.

3 Bake 25 to 30 minutes or until top is golden brown and knife inserted in center comes out clean. Let stand 5 minutes before serving. Spread 2 tablespoons mayonnaise over top of pie. Sprinkle with lettuce; top with tomato.

1 SERVING: Calories 350; Total Fat 28g (Saturated Fat 8g; Trans Fat 0g); Cholesterol 110mg; Sodium 620mg; Total Carbohydrate 10g (Dietary Fiber 0g); Protein 14g **Exchanges:** $\frac{1}{2}$ Starch, 2 High-Fat Meat, 2$\frac{1}{2}$ Fat **Carbohydrate Choices:** $\frac{1}{2}$

Quick Tip: Cut down on prep time by purchasing a bag of shredded lettuce.

Impossibly Easy Dijon-Wild Rice Pie

PREP TIME: 15 MINUTES • START TO FINISH: 55 MINUTES
6 SERVINGS

½ cup cooked wild rice

1 cup cubed cooked ham

½ cup chopped red bell pepper

1 cup shredded Swiss cheese (4 oz)

⅔ cup Original Bisquick mix

⅛ teaspoon pepper

1 cup milk

⅓ cup chive-and-onion sour cream potato topper (from 12-oz container)

1 tablespoon country-style Dijon mustard

2 eggs

3 tablespoons sliced almonds

Fresh chives, if desired

1 Heat oven to 400°F. Spray 9-inch glass pie plate with cooking spray. Layer wild rice, ham, bell pepper, and cheese in pie plate.

2 In medium bowl, mix remaining ingredients except almonds and chives with whisk or fork until blended. Pour over ingredients in pie plate. Sprinkle with almonds.

3 Bake 30 to 35 minutes or until knife inserted in center comes out clean. Let stand 5 minutes before serving. Garnish with chives.

1 SERVING: Calories 270; Total Fat 15g (Saturated Fat 7g; Trans Fat 0.5g); Cholesterol 105mg; Sodium 730mg; Total Carbohydrate 17g (Dietary Fiber 1g); Protein 16g **Exchanges:** ½ Starch, ½ Low-Fat Milk, 1½ Lean Meat, 1½ Fat **Carbohydrate Choices:** 1

Quick Tip: There's no need to cook wild rice for this dish. Look for it already cooked in cans or in the frozen foods department.

Gluten Free Oven-Baked Chicken

PREP TIME: 10 MINUTES • START TO FINISH: 1 HOUR
5 SERVINGS

**1 tablespoon butter
  or margarine**

1 cup Bisquick Gluten Free mix

1 teaspoon seasoned salt

1 teaspoon paprika

¹/₂ teaspoon garlic powder

¹/₄ teaspoon pepper

2 eggs, beaten

1 cut-up whole chicken (3 lb)

1 Heat oven to 400°F. In 13×9-inch (3-quart) glass baking dish, melt butter in oven. In medium bowl, stir Bisquick mix, salt, paprika, garlic powder and pepper. Place eggs in shallow dish.

2 Dip chicken into eggs, then coat with Bisquick mixture; repeat dipping in eggs and Bisquick mixture. Place skin side down in heated dish.

3 Bake 35 minutes. Turn chicken; bake about 15 minutes longer or until juice is clear when thickest part is cut to bone (170°F for breasts; 180°F for thighs and drumsticks).

1 SERVING: Calories 420; Total Fat 21g (Saturated Fat 7g; Trans Fat 0.5g); Cholesterol 195mg; Sodium 680mg; Total Carbohydrate 21g (Dietary Fiber 0g); Protein 36g **Exchanges:** 1¹/₂ Starch, 4¹/₂ Lean Meat, 1¹/₂ Fat **Carbohydrate Choices:** 1¹/₂

Quick Tip: Plan to serve this easy chicken with baked sweet potatoes that can bake at the same time as the chicken. Just add your favorite frozen veggie and you've got a fabulous meal.

Gluten Free Ultimate Chicken Fingers

PREP TIME: 25 MINUTES   **START TO FINISH: 25 MINUTES**
5 SERVINGS

³/₄ **cup Bisquick Gluten Free mix**

¹/₂ **cup grated Parmesan cheese**

1 teaspoon paprika

¹/₂ **teaspoon salt or garlic salt**

2 eggs

3 boneless skinless chicken breasts (1 lb), cut crosswise into ¹/₂**-inch strips**

3 tablespoons butter or margarine, melted

1 Heat oven to 450°F. Line cookie sheet with foil; spray with cooking spray. In shallow dish, stir Bisquick mix, cheese, paprika and salt. In another shallow dish, beat eggs slightly.

2 Dip chicken strips into eggs, then coat with Bisquick mixture; repeat dipping in eggs and Bisquick mixture. Place chicken on cookie sheet. Drizzle butter over chicken.

3 Bake 12 to 14 minutes, turning after 6 minutes, until no longer pink in center.

1 SERVING: Calories 310; Total Fat 15g (Saturated Fat 8g; Trans Fat 0g); Cholesterol 165mg; Sodium 740mg; Total Carbohydrate 16g (Dietary Fiber 0g); Protein 28g **Exchanges:** 1 Starch, 3 ¹/₂ Lean Meat, 1 Fat **Carbohydrate Choices:** 1

Almond- and Peach-Crusted Pork Chops

PREP TIME: 30 MINUTES • **START TO FINISH: 30 MINUTES**
6 SERVINGS

1 egg

2 tablespoons peach preserves

¹/₂ cup Original Bisquick mix

¹/₂ cup coarsely chopped
   sliced almonds

1 tablespoon cornmeal

¹/₂ teaspoon salt

6 boneless pork loin chops,
   ¹/₂ inch thick (1¹/₂ lb)

1 tablespoon vegetable oil

Chopped fresh parsley,
   if desired

1 In shallow dish, beat egg and preserves with fork, breaking apart any large pieces of preserves. In another shallow dish, mix Bisquick mix, almonds, cornmeal and salt. Dip pork chops into egg mixture, then coat with Bisquick mixture.

2 In 12-inch nonstick skillet, heat oil over medium-low heat. Add pork chops; cook 15 to 18 minutes, turning once, until crust is golden brown and pork is no longer pink in center. Sprinkle with parsley. Serve immediately.

1 SERVING: Calories 320; Total Fat 18g (Saturated Fat 4g; Trans Fat 0g); Cholesterol 105mg; Sodium 310mg; Total Carbohydrate 12g (Dietary Fiber 1g); Protein 28g **Exchanges:** 1 Starch, 3¹/₂ Lean Meat, 1 Fat **Carbohydrate Choices:** 1

Quick Tip: For an easy, special touch, heat additional peach preserves until melted and drizzle over the chops.

Italian Breaded Pork Chops

PREP TIME: 10 MINUTES   START TO FINISH: 25 MINUTES
4 SERVINGS

½ cup Original Bisquick mix

⅓ cup Italian dressing

½ cup garlic-herb dry
   bread crumbs

6 boneless pork loin chops,
   ½ inch thick (1 lb)

2 tablespoons vegetable oil

Chopped fresh parsley,
   if desired

1 In 3 separate shallow dishes, place Bisquick mix, dressing and bread crumbs. Coat pork chops with Bisquick mix. Dip coated pork chops into dressing, then coat with bread crumbs.

2 In 12-inch nonstick skillet, heat oil over medium-high heat. Add pork; cook about 5 minutes or until golden brown. Reduce heat to low; carefully turn pork. Cook 10 to 15 minutes longer or until pork is no longer pink in center. Sprinkle with parsley. Serve immediately.

1 SERVING: Calories 510; Total Fat 31g (Saturated Fat 7g; Trans Fat 0g); Cholesterol 110mg; Sodium 720mg; Total Carbohydrate 20g (Dietary Fiber 0g); Protein 40g **Exchanges:** 1½ Starch, 5 Lean Meat, 3 Fat **Carbohydrate Choices:** 1

Quick Tip: It's easy to cook some spaghetti while the chops are cooking. Serve it with the chops, and drizzle warm pasta sauce over spaghetti and chops.

Spiced Tilapia with Honeyed Mango-Lime Sauce

PREP TIME: 30 MINUTES   START TO FINISH: 30 MINUTES
4 SERVINGS

SAUCE

1 ripe mango, seed removed, peeled and diced

Grated peel and juice of 1 medium lime

2 green onions, coarsely chopped (2 tablespoons)

1 tablespoon honey

½ teaspoon kosher (coarse) salt

FISH

1 egg

2 tablespoons milk

1 cup Original Bisquick mix

½ teaspoon kosher (coarse) salt

¼ teaspoon freshly ground pepper

4 tilapia fillets (1 lb)

¼ cup vegetable or canola oil

1 teaspoon chili paste

1 tablespoon chopped fresh cilantro

1 In food processor, place all sauce ingredients. Cover; process until smooth. Set aside until serving time.

2 In shallow dish, beat egg and milk with fork. In another shallow dish, mix Bisquick mix, salt and pepper. Dip fish in egg mixture, then coat with Bisquick mixture.

3 In 12-inch skillet, heat oil and chili paste over medium heat; stir to combine. Add fish; cook 4 to 6 minutes, turning once, until golden brown and fish flakes easily with fork.

4 To serve, place fish on serving platter or individual plates. Drizzle evenly with sauce; sprinkle with cilantro.

1 SERVING: Calories 430; Total Fat 20g (Saturated Fat 4g; Trans Fat 1g); Cholesterol 115mg; Sodium 1090mg; Total Carbohydrate 35g (Dietary Fiber 2g); Protein 26g **Exchanges:** 1½ Starch, 1 Other Carbohydrate, 3 Lean Meat, 2 Fat **Carbohydrate Choices:** 2

This spicy-sweet fish dish has dining-out elegance with dining-in ease. The crisp tilapia fillets are cooled by a tangy mango sauce.

BETTER WITH BISQUICK

Contest Winner:

Veronica Callaghan • Glastonbury, CT

This recipe won 2nd place in our Better with Bisquick Contest.

Basil-Breaded Fish Fillets

PREP TIME: 20 MINUTES • START TO FINISH: 20 MINUTES
4 SERVINGS

1 lb fish fillets, about ¹/₂ inch thick

2 tablespoons olive or vegetable oil

¹/₂ cup Bisquick Heart Smart mix

¹/₄ cup garlic-herb dry bread crumbs

1 tablespoon chopped fresh or 1 teaspoon dried basil leaves

¹/₄ teaspoon salt

1 egg

1 Cut fish into 4 serving pieces. In 10-inch skillet, heat oil over medium heat.

2 In small shallow dish, mix Bisquick mix, bread crumbs, basil and salt. In another shallow dish, beat egg with fork. Dip fish into egg, then coat with Bisquick mixture.

3 Reduce heat to medium-low. Add fish; cook 8 to 10 minutes, turning once, until fish flakes easily with fork and is brown on both sides.

1 SERVING: Calories 240; Total Fat 9g (Saturated Fat 1.5g; Trans Fat 0g); Cholesterol 115mg; Sodium 480mg; Total Carbohydrate 15g (Dietary Fiber 0g); Protein 25g **Exchanges:** 1 Starch, 3 Lean Meat **Carbohydrate Choices:** 1

Quick Tip: It's quick—and easy—to make a delicious sauce to serve with the fish. Just mix ¹/₂ cup mayonnaise or salad dressing and 2 tablespoons basil pesto. Then, garnish with lemon wedges and fresh basil.

Sassy Fish Bake with Tomato-Bacon-Avocado Salsa

PREP TIME: 25 MINUTES • START TO FINISH: 45 MINUTES
6 SERVINGS

FISH BAKE

1 cup Original Bisquick mix

¹/₂ to 1 teaspoon salt, if desired

1 teaspoon smoked Spanish paprika

¹/₂ to 1 teaspoon chipotle chile powder

¹/₂ teaspoon lemon-pepper seasoning

¹/₂ cup evaporated milk or 2 egg whites mixed with 2 teaspoons water

6 tilapia fillets (1¹/₂ lb)

Cooking spray

SALSA

4 slices smoked thick-sliced bacon, crisply cooked, crumbled

2 avocados, pitted, peeled and chopped

2 cups diced seeded tomatoes (about 2 large)

¹/₃ cup chopped red onion

¹/₄ cup chopped fresh cilantro

2 tablespoons lime juice

¹/₂ teaspoon salt

¹/₄ teaspoon freshly ground pepper

1 Heat oven to 375°F. Spray 13×9-inch (3-quart) glass baking dish with cooking spray. In shallow dish, mix Bisquick mix, salt, paprika, chile powder and lemon-pepper seasoning. In another shallow dish, place evaporated milk.

2 Dip fish in milk, then coat with Bisquick mixture (discard any remaining mixture). Place fish in baking dish. Spray tops of fish with cooking spray to moisten.

3 Bake uncovered 15 to 20 minutes or until fish flakes easily with fork. Meanwhile, in large bowl, mix all salsa ingredients. Let stand 10 to 15 minutes. Stir well; taste and adjust seasoning as needed.

4 To serve, place fish on 6 warm plates; top each with a spoonful of salsa.

1 SERVING: Calories 340; Total Fat 15g (Saturated Fat 3.5g; Trans Fat 1g); Cholesterol 70mg; Sodium 740mg; Total Carbohydrate 22g (Dietary Fiber 5g); Protein 28g **Exchanges:** 1¹/₂ Starch, 3 Medium-Fat Meat **Carbohydrate Choices:** 1¹/₂

BETTER WITH BISQUICK

Contest Winner:

Peter Halferty • Corpus Christi, TX

This recipe won honorable mention in our Better with Bisquick Contest.

Beer-Battered Fish

PREP TIME: 15 MINUTES   **START TO FINISH: 15 MINUTES**
4 SERVINGS

Vegetable oil for deep frying

1 lb fish fillets, thawed if frozen

3 to 4 tablespoons Original Bisquick mix

1 cup Original Bisquick mix

1/2 cup regular or nonalcoholic beer

1/2 teaspoon salt

1 egg

Tartar sauce, if desired

1 In heavy 3-quart saucepan or deep fryer, heat oil (1½ inches) to 350°F. Lightly coat fish with 3 to 4 tablespoons Bisquick mix.

2 In medium bowl, beat 1 cup Bisquick mix, the beer, salt and egg with whisk or fork until smooth. (If batter is too thick, stir in additional beer, 1 tablespoon at a time, until desired consistency.) Dip fish into batter, letting excess drip into bowl.

3 Fry fish in oil about 2 minutes on each side or until golden brown; drain. Serve hot with tartar sauce.

1 SERVING: Calories 300; Total Fat 10g (Saturated Fat 2.5g; Trans Fat 1.5g); Cholesterol 115mg; Sodium 890mg; Total Carbohydrate 26g (Dietary Fiber 1g); Protein 26g **Exchanges:** 2 Starch, 2½ Lean Meat, ½ Fat **Carbohydrate Choices:** 2

Quick Tip: For a quick meal idea, serve the fillets in burger buns with tangy tartar sauce, crisp lettuce leaves and tomato slices. Deli coleslaw is another great addition to the meal.

Chili Chicken Soup with Cilantro Dumplings

PREP TIME: 25 MINUTES   START TO FINISH: 45 MINUTES
5 SERVINGS (1 CUP SOUP AND 2 DUMPLINGS EACH)

SOUP

1 tablespoon vegetable oil

1¼ lb boneless skinless chicken breasts, cut into 1-inch cubes

1 medium onion, chopped (½ cup)

3 teaspoons chili powder

½ to 1 teaspoon salt

5 cups chicken broth

DUMPLINGS

2 cups Original Bisquick mix

⅔ cup milk

½ cup chopped fresh cilantro

½ teaspoon ground cumin

1 jalapeño chile, seeded, chopped, if desired

1 In 3-quart saucepan, heat oil over medium heat. Add chicken, onion, chili powder and salt; cook, stirring frequently, until chicken is browned. Stir in broth. Heat to boiling. Reduce heat to medium; simmer uncovered 5 minutes.

2 Meanwhile, in medium bowl, mix Bisquick mix and milk until soft dough forms. Fold in cilantro, cumin and chile.

3 Drop dough by 10 rounded tablespoonfuls onto simmering soup. Cook uncovered 10 minutes. Cover; cook 10 minutes longer.

1 SERVING: Calories 400; Total Fat 13g (Saturated Fat 3.5g; Trans Fat 2g); Cholesterol 75mg; Sodium 1770mg; Total Carbohydrate 36g (Dietary Fiber 2g); Protein 33g **Exchanges:** 2½ Starch, 3½ Lean Meat **Carbohydrate Choices:** 2½

BETTER with BISQUICK

Contest Winner:

Greg Fontenot • The Woodlands, TX

This recipe won honorable mention in our Better with Bisquick Contest.

"Classic favorite with a Hispanic twist."

Gluten Free Chicken and Dumplings

PREP TIME: 20 MINUTES   START TO FINISH: 45 MINUTES
4 SERVINGS

CHICKEN

1½ cups cut-up cooked chicken

1 cup frozen mixed vegetables

1 teaspoon seasoned salt

¼ teaspoon pepper

2½ cups chicken broth

1 cup milk

3 tablespoons cornstarch

DUMPLINGS

¾ cup Bisquick Gluten Free mix

⅓ cup milk

2 tablespoons butter or margarine, melted

1 egg

1 tablespoon chopped fresh parsley

1 In 3-quart saucepan, heat chicken, vegetables, salt, pepper and broth to boiling. In small bowl, mix 1 cup milk and the cornstarch with whisk or fork until smooth; stir into chicken mixture. Heat just to boiling.

2 In small bowl, stir dumpling ingredients with fork until blended. Gently drop dough by 8 rounded tablespoonfuls onto boiling chicken mixture.

3 Cook uncovered over low heat 10 minutes. Cover; cook 15 minutes longer.

1 SERVING: Calories 360; Total Fat 14g (Saturated Fat 6g; Trans Fat 0g); Cholesterol 120mg; Sodium 1390mg; Total Carbohydrate 36g (Dietary Fiber 2g); Protein 24g **Exchanges:** 1½ Starch, ½ Other Carbohydrate, ½ Vegetable, 2½ Lean Meat, 1 Fat **Carbohydrate Choices:** 2½

Quick Tip: You can use 1 cup of cut green beans, peas, or corn in place of the mixed vegetables.

CHAPTER 5

Delectable

Desserts

Spiced Apple Cupcakes with Salted Caramel Frosting

PREP TIME: 30 MINUTES   START TO FINISH: 1 HOUR 25 MINUTES
12 CUPCAKES

CUPCAKES

1½ **cups Original Bisquick mix**

½ **cup sugar**

1 **teaspoon apple pie spice**

½ **cup apple cider or juice**

2 **tablespoons butter or shortening, softened**

1 **teaspoon vanilla**

1 **egg**

1¼ **cups chopped peeled apple (about 1 medium)**

SALTED CARAMEL FROSTING

¾ **cup vanilla creamy ready-to-spread frosting**

¼ **cup caramel topping**

¼ **teaspoon kosher (coarse) salt**

1 Heat oven to 375°F. Place paper baking cup in each of 12 regular-size muffin cups. In large bowl, beat all cupcake ingredients except apple with electric mixer on low speed 30 seconds, scraping bowl constantly. Beat on medium speed 4 minutes, scraping bowl occasionally. Fold in apple. Divide batter evenly among muffin cups, filling each about three-fourths full.

2 Bake 17 to 22 minutes or until toothpick inserted in center comes out clean. Immediately remove cupcakes from pan to cooling rack. Cool completely, about 30 minutes.

3 In small bowl, mix frosting and caramel topping until smooth and spreadable. Frost cupcakes. Sprinkle with kosher salt.

1 CUPCAKE: Calories 220; Total Fat 7g (Saturated Fat 2.5g; Trans Fat 1.5g); Cholesterol 25mg; Sodium 310mg; Total Carbohydrate 37g (Dietary Fiber 0g); Protein 1g **Exchanges:** 1 Starch, 1½ Other Carbohydrate, 1½ Fat **Carbohydrate Choices:** 2½

BETTER WITH BISQUICK

Contest Winner:

Edwina Gadsby • Great Falls, MT
This decadent dessert won honorable mention in our Better with Bisquick Contest.

This recipe was inspired by my latest obsession—salted caramels! I decided to combine it with another one of my all-time favorite treats— cupcakes. Apples and caramel are a marriage made in heaven.

Cream Cheese Pound Cake

PREP TIME: 15 MINUTES   **START TO FINISH: 2 HOURS 20 MINUTES**

10 SERVINGS

3 cups Original Bisquick mix

1¹⁄₂ cups granulated sugar

³⁄₄ cup butter or margarine, softened

¹⁄₂ cup all-purpose flour

¹⁄₈ teaspoon salt

1 teaspoon vanilla

6 eggs

1 package (8 oz) cream cheese, softened

Powdered sugar, if desired

Fruit for garnish, if desired

1 Heat oven to 350°F. Grease 12-cup fluted tube cake pan or 2 (9×5-inch) loaf pans with shortening; lightly flour. In large bowl, beat all ingredients except powdered sugar with electric mixer on low speed 30 seconds, scraping bowl frequently. Beat on medium speed 4 minutes, scraping bowl occasionally. Pour into pan.

2 Bake 55 to 60 minutes or until toothpick inserted near center comes out clean. Cool 5 minutes. Turn pan upside down onto cooling rack or heatproof serving plate; remove pan. Cool cake completely, about 1 hour. Sprinkle with powdered sugar and serve with fruit, if desired.

1 SERVING: Calories 540; Total Fat 29g (Saturated Fat 15g; Trans Fat 2g); Cholesterol 190mg; Sodium 740mg; Total Carbohydrate 59g (Dietary Fiber 1g); Protein 8g **Exchanges:** 2 Starch, 2 Other Carbohydrate, 5¹⁄₂ Fat **Carbohydrate Choices:** 4

Orange Dream Cake

PREP TIME: 25 MINUTES   START TO FINISH: 3 HOURS 5 MINUTES
8 SERVINGS

TOPPING

1 box (4-serving size) white chocolate or vanilla instant pudding and pie filling mix

1 cup milk

1 cup frozen (thawed) whipped topping

1 can (11 oz) mandarin orange segments, well drained

CAKE

1½ cups Original Bisquick mix

½ cup sugar

⅓ cup milk

2 tablespoons butter or margarine, softened

1 teaspoon grated orange peel

½ teaspoon vanilla

2 eggs

½ cup grated white chocolate baking bars

GARNISH

Whipped topping

Toasted slivered almonds, if desired*

White chocolate curls, if desired

1 In medium bowl, beat pudding mix and 1 cup milk with whisk or electric mixer on low speed about 2 minutes or until well blended. Fold in whipped topping. Reserve about 8 orange segments for garnish; stir remaining orange segments into pudding mixture. Cover; refrigerate 1 hour.

2 Meanwhile, heat oven to 350°F. Grease bottom and side of 9-inch round cake pan with shortening or cooking spray; lightly flour.

3 In medium bowl, beat all cake ingredients except white chocolate with electric mixer on low speed 30 seconds, scraping bowl constantly. Beat on medium speed 4 minutes, scraping bowl occasionally. Stir in white chocolate. Pour into pan.

4 Bake about 30 minutes or until toothpick inserted in center comes out clean. Cool 10 minutes. Remove from pan to cooling rack. Cool completely, about 1 hour.

5 Place cake on serving plate. Spoon whipped topping onto cake. Garnish with reserved orange segments, the almonds and chocolate curls. Store covered in refrigerator.

1 SERVING: Calories 380; Total Fat 15g (Saturated Fat 8g; Trans Fat 1g); Cholesterol 65mg; Sodium 520mg; Total Carbohydrate 55g (Dietary Fiber 1g); Protein 6g **Exchanges:** 1 Starch, 2½ Other Carbohydrate, ½ High-Fat Meat, 2 Fat **Carbohydrate Choices:** 3½

*Toast nuts in a 350°F oven about 10 minutes, stirring occasionally, until golden brown. Or, sprinkle nuts in an ungreased heavy skillet. Cook over medium-low heat 5 to 7 minutes, stirring frequently, until browning begins, then stir constantly until golden brown. Watch carefully; time varies greatly between gas and electric cooktops.

Gluten Free Impossibly Easy French Apple Pie

PREP TIME: 25 MINUTES   START TO FINISH: 1 HOUR 15 MINUTES
6 SERVINGS

FILLING

3 cups thinly sliced peeled apples (3 medium)

1 teaspoon ground cinnamon

$^1/_4$ teaspoon ground nutmeg

$^1/_2$ cup Bisquick Gluten Free mix

$^1/_2$ cup granulated sugar

$^1/_2$ cup milk

2 tablespoons butter or margarine, melted

3 eggs

STREUSEL

$^1/_3$ cup Bisquick Gluten Free mix

$^1/_3$ cup chopped nuts

$^1/_4$ cup packed brown sugar

3 tablespoons cold butter or margarine

1 Heat oven to 325°F. Spray 9-inch glass pie plate with cooking spray. In medium bowl, mix apples, cinnamon and nutmeg; place in pie plate.

2 In medium bowl, stir remaining filling ingredients until well blended. Pour over apple mixture in pie plate. In small bowl, mix all streusel ingredients with fork until coarse crumbs; sprinkle over filling.

3 Bake 45 to 50 minutes or until knife inserted in center comes out clean. Store in refrigerator.

1 SERVING: Calories 380; Total Fat 17g (Saturated Fat 8g; Trans Fat 0g); Cholesterol 135mg; Sodium 300mg; Total Carbohydrate 49g (Dietary Fiber 2g); Protein 6g **Exchanges:** 1$^1/_2$ Starch, 2 Other Carbohydrate, 3 Fat **Carbohydrate Choices:** 3

Quick Tip: Top this decadent pie with gluten free whipped cream or ice cream.

Citrus Mini Cheesecakes

PREP TIME: 15 MINUTES   START TO FINISH: 1 HOUR 55 MINUTES
60 MINI CHEESECAKES

CRUST

1¹/₂ cups Original Bisquick mix

¹/₂ cup sugar

1 teaspoon grated lime, lemon or orange peel

¹/₃ cup cold butter or margarine

FILLING

3 packages (8 oz each) cream cheese, softened

1¹/₂ cups sugar

2 tablespoons Original Bisquick mix

1 teaspoon grated lime, lemon or orange peel

1¹/₄ cups milk

3 tablespoons lime, lemon or orange juice

1 teaspoon vanilla

3 eggs

GARNISH

Thinly sliced lime, lemon, or orange wedges, if desired

1 Heat oven to 375°F. In medium bowl, mix all crust ingredients except butter. With pastry blender (or pulling 2 table knives through ingredients in opposite directions), cut in butter until mixture looks like coarse crumbs. Pat in bottom of ungreased 15×10×1-inch pan. Bake 10 minutes.

2 Meanwhile, in large bowl, beat cream cheese, 1½ cups sugar, 2 tablespoons Bisquick mix and 1 teaspoon of the lime peel with electric mixer on medium speed until blended and fluffy. On low speed, beat in remaining filling ingredients until blended. Beat on low speed 2 minutes longer.

3 Pour filling over partially baked crust. Bake 35 to 40 minutes or until knife inserted in center comes out clean. Cool completely, about 1 hour. Refrigerate until ready to serve. For mini cheesecakes, cut into 10 rows by 6 rows. Garnish with fruit wedges, if desired. Store covered in refrigerator.

1 MINI CHEESECAKE: Calories 100; Total Fat 6g (Saturated Fat 3.5g; Trans Fat 0g); Cholesterol 25mg; Sodium 85mg; Total Carbohydrate 9g (Dietary Fiber 0g); Protein 2g **Exchanges:** ¹/₂ Other Carbohydrate, 1¹/₂ Fat Carbohydrate Choices: ¹/₂

Quick Tip: To make cutting the bars easier, use a knife dipped in a glass of water. Clean the knife and dip again in water when needed.

Strawberry-Banana Crepes

PREP TIME: 25 MINUTES • **START TO FINISH: 45 MINUTES**
ABOUT 12 CREPES

CREPES

1 cup Original Bisquick mix

³/₄ **cup milk**

2 eggs

FILLING

1¹/₂ cups whipping cream

¹/₄ **cup sugar**

2 to 3 bananas, sliced

TOPPING

Whipped cream

1 pint (2 cups) fresh strawberries, sliced, or 1 box (10 oz) frozen strawberries, partially thawed

¹/₄ **cup chopped walnuts**

1 In small bowl, stir crepe ingredients until blended.

2 Grease 6- or 7-inch nonstick skillet with shortening; heat over medium heat until bubbly. For each crepe, pour 2 tablespoons batter into skillet; immediately rotate skillet until batter covers bottom. Cook until golden brown on bottom side. Run wide spatula around edge to loosen; turn and cook other side until golden brown. Stack crepes as removed from skillet, placing waxed paper between each; keep covered.

3 In chilled medium bowl, beat whipping cream and sugar with electric mixer on high speed until stiff peaks form.

4 To assemble each crepe, spoon about 3 tablespoons whipped cream down center of each crepe. Top each with 4 or 5 banana slices; roll up. Top each crepe with whipped cream, strawberries and walnuts.

1 CREPE: Calories 220; Total Fat 14g (Saturated Fat 7g; Trans Fat 0.5g); Cholesterol 70mg; Sodium 150mg; Total Carbohydrate 19g (Dietary Fiber 1g); Protein 4g **Exchanges:** 1 Starch, ¹/₂ Other Carbohydrate, 2¹/₂ Fat **Carbohydrate Choices:** 1

Quick Tip: Crepes can be frozen up to 3 months. Stack cool, unfilled crepes with waxed paper between. Wrap in foil or place in a resealable plastic freezer bag; label and freeze. Thaw at room temperature about 1 hour or in refrigerator 6 to 8 hours.

Fresh Lemon Cream Crepes

**PREP TIME: 45 MINUTES • START TO FINISH: 45 MINUTES
ABOUT 10 CREPES**

CREPES

½ **cup Original Bisquick mix**

1 **tablespoon granulated sugar**

½ **cup milk**

1 **tablespoon butter, melted**

2 **eggs**

FILLING

2 **cups sour cream**

½ **cup milk**

1 **tablespoon grated lemon peel**

¼ **cup fresh lemon juice**

1 **box (4-serving size) vanilla instant pudding and pie filling mix**

2 **cups fresh raspberries**

GARNISH

Powdered sugar

Additional fresh raspberries, if desired

1 In small bowl, beat Bisquick mix, sugar, ½ cup milk, the butter and eggs with whisk or fork until blended.

2 Grease 6- or 7-inch nonstick skillet with shortening; heat over medium heat until bubbly. For each crepe, pour 2 tablespoons batter into skillet; immediately rotate skillet until batter covers bottom. Cook until golden brown on bottom side. Run wide spatula around edge to loosen; turn and cook other side until golden brown. Stack crepes as removed from skillet, placing waxed paper between each; keep covered.

3 In small bowl, beat sour cream, ½ milk, the lemon peel, lemon juice and pudding mix with whisk or fork until blended.

4 To assemble each crepe, spoon about ¼ cup of the filling on one end of crepe; top with 5 raspberries. Roll up; sprinkle each crepe with powdered sugar. Serve with additional raspberries and sprinkle with powdered sugar.

1 CREPE: Calories 240; Total Fat 14g (Saturated Fat 8g; Trans Fat 0.5g); Cholesterol 75mg; Sodium 300mg; Total Carbohydrate 23g (Dietary Fiber 2g); Protein 5g **Exchanges:** 1 Starch, ½ Fruit, 2½ Fat **Carbohydrate Choices:** 1½

Quick Tip: Not enough time to make the crepes start to finish? Filling and crepes can be made up to 4 hours ahead, covered and refrigerated separately before assembly. Then all you have to do is assemble and serve!

Banana-Coconut Cream Dessert

PREP TIME: 15 MINUTES ▪ **START TO FINISH: 2 HOURS**
16 SERVINGS

2 cups Original Bisquick mix

2 tablespoons sugar

$\frac{1}{4}$ cup cold butter or margarine

1 package (4-serving size) vanilla instant pudding and pie filling mix

1$\frac{3}{4}$ cups milk

2 medium bananas, sliced

2 cups whipped cream

$\frac{1}{2}$ cup toasted shredded coconut*

1 Heat oven to 375°F. In medium bowl, mix Bisquick mix and sugar. Using pastry blender (or pulling 2 table knives through mixture in opposite directions), cut in butter until mixture looks like coarse crumbs. Press in bottom of ungreased 9-inch square pan.

2 Bake about 15 minutes or until light brown. Cool completely, about 30 minutes.

3 Make pudding mix as directed on package for pudding, using 1¾ cups milk; spread over crust. Top with banana slices. Spread whipped cream over top. Sprinkle with coconut. Cover; refrigerate at least 1 hour but no longer than 24 hours before serving.

1 SERVING: Calories 250; Total Fat 16g (Saturated Fat 10g; Trans Fat 1g); Cholesterol 45mg; Sodium 320mg; Total Carbohydrate 23g (Dietary Fiber 1g); Protein 3g **Exchanges:** ½ Starch, 1 Other Carbohydrate, 3 Fat **Carbohydrate Choices:** 1½

*To toast coconut, spread on ungreased cookie sheet and bake at 350°F for 10 to 15 minutes, stirring occasionally, until coconut is light golden brown.

Strawberry Shortcake Squares

PREP TIME: 30 MINUTES · START TO FINISH: 2 HOURS 5 MINUTES
15 SERVINGS

CAKE

3 cups Original Bisquick mix

1 cup granulated sugar

¹⁄₄ cup butter or margarine, softened

1 cup milk

2 teaspoons vanilla

2 eggs

TOPPING

1 cup whipping cream

1 package (8 oz) cream cheese, softened

¹⁄₃ cup powdered sugar

1 teaspoon vanilla

6 cups sliced fresh strawberries (about 2 lb)

1 Heat oven to 350°F. Grease bottom and sides of 13×9-inch pan with shortening and lightly flour, or spray pan with baking spray with flour. In large bowl, beat cake ingredients with electric mixer on low speed 30 seconds, scraping bowl occasionally. Pour into pan.

2 Bake 30 to 35 minutes or until toothpick inserted in center comes out clean. Cool completely, about 1 hour.

3 Meanwhile, in chilled small bowl, beat whipping cream on high speed until soft peaks form; set aside. In medium bowl, beat cream cheese, powdered sugar and vanilla on medium speed until well blended. Fold in whipped cream.

4 Frost top of cooled cake with whipped cream mixture. If desired, frosted cake can be refrigerated up to 6 hours. To serve, cut cake into squares; place on individual dessert plates. Top with strawberries.

1 SERVING: Calories 340; Total Fat 18g (Saturated Fat 10g; Trans Fat 1.5g); Cholesterol 75mg; Sodium 380mg; Total Carbohydrate 38g (Dietary Fiber 2g); Protein 5g **Exchanges:** 1¹⁄₂ Starch, ¹⁄₂ Fruit, ¹⁄₂ Other Carbohydrate, 3¹⁄₂ Fat **Carbohydrate Choices:** 2¹⁄₂

Gluten Free Strawberry Shortcakes

PREP TIME: 10 MINUTES   **START TO FINISH: 30 MINUTES**
6 SERVINGS

4 cups (1 quart) strawberries, sliced

¹/₂ cup sugar

2 ¹/₃ cups Bisquick Gluten Free mix

¹/₃ cup butter or margarine

³/₄ cup milk

¹/₂ teaspoon vanilla

3 eggs, beaten

³/₄ cup whipping cream, whipped

1 In small bowl, mix strawberries and ¼ cup of the sugar; set aside. Heat oven to 425°F. Grease cookie sheet with shortening or cooking spray.

2 In medium bowl, mix Bisquick mix and remaining ¼ cup sugar. Using pastry blender (or pulling 2 table knives through ingredients in opposite directions), cut in butter until mixture looks like coarse crumbs. Stir in milk, vanilla and eggs. Drop by 6 rounded tablespoonfuls onto cookie sheet, 3 inches apart.

3 Bake 10 to 12 minutes or until light golden brown. Cool 5 minutes. With serrated knife, split shortcakes; fill and top with strawberries and whipped cream.

1 SERVING: Calories 520; Total Fat 24g (Saturated Fat 13g; Trans Fat 1g); Cholesterol 170mg; Sodium 650mg; Total Carbohydrate 67g (Dietary Fiber 3g); Protein 8g **Exchanges:** 1¹/₂ Starch, 2 Fruit, 1 Other Carbohydrate, ¹/₂ High-Fat Meat, 4 Fat **Carbohydrate Choices:** 4¹/₂

Quick Tip: For the best results, always slice strawberries just before using. Raspberries are a yummy substitution for the strawberries.

Pecan-Cinnamon Shortcakes with Bananas and Dulce de Leche

PREP TIME: 20 MINUTES • **START TO FINISH: 1 HOUR 10 MINUTES**
4 SERVINGS

1¼ cups Original Bisquick mix

2 tablespoons sugar

¼ cup finely chopped pecans

½ teaspoon ground cinnamon

1½ cups heavy whipping cream, chilled

½ teaspoon sugar

4 tablespoons dulce de leche (caramelized sweetened condensed milk), from 13.4-oz can

2 ripe bananas, cut into ¼-inch slices

4 teaspoons grated chocolate

1 Heat oven to 350°F. In medium bowl, mix Bisquick mix, 2 tablespoons sugar, the pecans and cinnamon. Add ½ cup of the cream; stir until soft dough forms.

2 Onto ungreased cookie sheet, drop dough by ¼ cupfuls 2 inches apart; pat into rounds, about ¾ inch thick. Sprinkle tops with ½ teaspoon sugar.

3 Bake 16 to 18 minutes or until light golden brown. Remove from cookie sheet to cooling rack. Cool completely, about 30 minutes.

4 In chilled large deep bowl, beat remaining 1 cup whipping cream with electric mixer on high speed until soft peaks form. Cover; refrigerate until serving time.

5 Using serrated knife, carefully slice shortcakes in half horizontally. Place bottom halves on 4 dessert plates; spread each with 1 tablespoon dulce de leche. Top each with ½ sliced banana, 3 tablespoons whipped cream and ½ teaspoon grated chocolate. Cover with top halves of shortcakes. Top each with 3 tablespoons whipped cream and ½ teaspoon grated chocolate. Serve immediately.

1 SERVING: Calories 640; Total Fat 40g (Saturated Fat 21g; Trans Fat 2.5g); Cholesterol 105mg; Sodium 510mg; Total Carbohydrate 63g (Dietary Fiber 3g); Protein 7g **Exchanges:** 2 Starch, 2 Other Carbohydrate, 8 Fat **Carbohydrate Choices:** 4

BETTER WITH BISQUICK

Contest Winner:

**Sherryl Vera •
Hurlburt Field, FL**
This decadent dessert won honorable mention in our Better with Bisquick Contest.

Caramel Apple Dessert

PREP TIME: 20 MINUTES   START TO FINISH: 1 HOUR 20 MINUTES
6 SERVINGS

1½ cups Original Bisquick mix

⅔ cup granulated sugar

½ cup milk

2 medium cooking apples, peeled, sliced (2 cups)

1 tablespoon lemon juice

¾ cup packed brown sugar

½ teaspoon ground cinnamon

1 cup boiling water

Ice cream or sweetened whipped cream, if desired

1 Heat oven to 350°F. In medium bowl, stir together Bisquick mix and granulated sugar. Stir in milk until blended.

2 Pour into ungreased 9-inch square pan. Top with apples; sprinkle with lemon juice. In small bowl, stir together brown sugar and cinnamon; sprinkle over apples. Pour boiling water over apples.

3 Bake 50 to 60 minutes or until toothpick inserted in center comes out clean. Spoon into small bowls. Serve warm with ice cream.

1 SERVING: Calories 350; Total Fat 4g (Saturated Fat 1.5g; Trans Fat 1g); Cholesterol 0mg; Sodium 390mg; Total Carbohydrate 74g (Dietary Fiber 1g); Protein 3g **Exchanges:** 1 Starch, 4 Other Carbohydrate, ½ Fat **Carbohydrate Choices:** 5

Quick Tip: To make yummy Caramel Pear Dessert Squares, substitute 2 cups sliced peeled pears for the apples.

Cherry and Peach Clafouti

PREP TIME: 15 MINUTES • START TO FINISH: 55 MINUTES
8 SERVINGS

1 can (14.5 oz) pitted tart
   red cherries in water,
   well drained
1 can (15.25 oz) sliced peaches
   in syrup, drained
$^{1}/_{3}$ cup slivered almonds
$^{2}/_{3}$ cup Original Bisquick mix
$^{1}/_{2}$ cup granulated sugar
1 cup milk
$1^{1}/_{2}$ teaspoons vanilla
3 eggs
1 teaspoon powdered sugar

1 Heat oven to 350°F. Spray 10-inch round shallow baking dish with cooking spray. Evenly distribute cherries, peaches and almonds in baking dish.

2 In medium bowl, beat Bisquick mix, granulated sugar, milk, vanilla and eggs with electric mixer on medium speed 2 minutes. Pour over fruit mixture.

3 Bake 35 to 40 minutes or until knife inserted in center comes out clean. Sprinkle with powdered sugar. Serve warm.

1 SERVING: Calories 230; Total Fat 6g (Saturated Fat 1.5g; Trans Fat 0g); Cholesterol 80mg; Sodium 170mg; Total Carbohydrate 37g (Dietary Fiber 2g); Protein 5g **Exchanges:** $^{1}/_{2}$ Fruit, 2 Other Carbohydrate, $^{1}/_{2}$ Medium-Fat Meat, $^{1}/_{2}$ Fat **Carbohydrate Choices:** $2^{1}/_{2}$

Blueberry-Peach Cobbler with Walnut Biscuits

PREP TIME: 30 MINUTES ▪ **START TO FINISH: 1 HOUR 40 MINUTES**
6 SERVINGS

FRUIT MIXTURE

8 medium fresh peaches (about 2 lb), peeled, each cut into 6 wedges

1 cup fresh blueberries

1 tablespoon cornstarch

$\frac{1}{2}$ cup granulated sugar

1 tablespoon lemon juice

$\frac{1}{4}$ teaspoon ground cinnamon

Dash salt

BISCUIT TOPPING

1 cup Original Bisquick mix

$\frac{1}{4}$ teaspoon ground nutmeg

2 tablespoons milk

2 tablespoons butter or margarine, softened

2 tablespoons granulated sugar

$\frac{2}{3}$ cup chopped walnuts

2 teaspoons milk, if desired

1 tablespoon coarse sugar, if desired

1 Heat oven to 400°F. In medium bowl, stir together fruit mixture ingredients; let stand 10 minutes to allow sugar to pull juices from peaches.

2 Transfer fruit mixture to ungreased 8-inch square (2-quart) glass baking dish. Bake uncovered about 10 minutes or until fruit is bubbling. Remove from oven; stir. Bake 10 to 12 minutes longer or until bubbly around edges (fruit must be hot in middle so biscuit topping bakes completely).

3 Meanwhile, in medium bowl, stir all biscuit topping ingredients except 2 teaspoons milk and coarse sugar until firm dough forms.

4 Drop dough by 6 rounded tablespoonfuls onto warm fruit mixture. Brush dough with 2 teaspoons milk. Sprinkle with coarse sugar.

5 Bake 25 to 30 minutes or until biscuits are deep golden brown and bottoms of biscuits are no longer doughy. Cool 10 minutes on cooling rack. Serve warm.

1 SERVING: Calories 380; Total Fat 15g (Saturated Fat 4g; Trans Fat 1g); Cholesterol 10mg; Sodium 300mg; Total Carbohydrate 55g (Dietary Fiber 4g); Protein 5g **Exchanges:** 1$\frac{1}{2}$ Starch, 1 Fruit, 1 Other Carbohydrate, 3 Fat **Carbohydrate Choices:** 3$\frac{1}{2}$

Quick Tip: Two bags (16 oz each) frozen sliced peaches, thawed, can be used in place of the fresh peaches, if you like.

Cherry-Raspberry Chocolate Cobbler

PREP TIME: 10 MINUTES • START TO FINISH: 40 MINUTES

8 SERVINGS

1 can (21 oz) cherry pie filling

1/2 teaspoon almond extract

2 cups fresh raspberries

3/4 cup chocolate ice cream

1/2 cup bittersweet chocolate chips

1 cup Original Bisquick mix

3 tablespoons sliced almonds

1 Heat oven to 375°F. In medium bowl, mix pie filling and extract; fold in raspberries. Spread in ungreased 8-inch square pan. Bake 15 minutes.

2 Meanwhile, in medium microwavable bowl, microwave ice cream and chocolate chips on High about 1 minute 30 seconds, stirring every 30 seconds, until smooth. Add Bisquick mix; mix well. Let stand until fruit is done baking.

3 Drop dough into 8 mounds (about 3 tablespoons each) onto hot fruit. Sprinkle almonds over each mound. Bake 15 to 18 minutes longer or until chocolate topping is just set. Serve warm.

1 SERVING: Calories 260; Total Fat 8g (Saturated Fat 3.5g; Trans Fat 0.5g); Cholesterol 0mg; Sodium 200mg; Total Carbohydrate 44g (Dietary Fiber 4g); Protein 3g **Exchanges:** 1/2 Starch, 1/2 Fruit, 2 Other Carbohydrate, 1 1/2 Fat **Carbohydrate Choices:** 3

BETTER WITH BISQUICK

Contest Winner:

Jeanne Holt • Mendota Heights, MN

This comforting dessert won honorable mention in our Better with Bisquick Contest.

Our family loves warm fruit cobbler and they love chocolate. So I combined the two and came up with this recipe.

Plum and Walnut Crisp

PREP TIME: 15 MINUTES • START TO FINISH: 1 HR 10 MINUTES
6 SERVINGS

6 medium red or purple plums, sliced (about 5 cups)

¾ cup sugar

3 tablespoons cornstarch

½ cup crushed gingersnap cookies (about 15 cookies)

½ cup chopped walnuts

½ cup Original Bisquick mix

¼ cup butter or margarine, softened

Ice cream, if desired

1 Heat oven to 350°F. Spray 8-inch square (2-quart) glass baking dish with cooking spray.

2 In large bowl, stir sliced plums, ½ cup of the sugar and the cornstarch until combined. Spread in baking dish.

3 In medium bowl, mix crushed cookies, walnuts, Bisquick mix, butter and remaining ¼ cup sugar with fork until crumbly. Sprinkle over plum mixture.

4 Bake 45 to 55 minutes or until mixture is hot and bubbly and topping is lightly browned. Serve warm, with ice cream if desired.

1 SERVING: Calories 410; Total Fat 17g (Saturated Fat 6g, Trans Fat 1g); Cholesterol 20mg; Sodium 260mg; Total Carbohydrate 60g (Dietary Fiber 3g); Protein 4g **Exchanges:** 1 Starch, 1 Fruit, 2 Other Carbohydrate, 3½ Fat **Carbohydrate Choices:** 4

Quick Tip: Crushed cinnamon-sugar graham crackers can be substituted for the gingersnap cookies.

Monster Oatmeal Cookies

PREP TIME: 50 MINUTES ◦ START TO FINISH: 50 MINUTES
ABOUT 1$\frac{1}{2}$ DOZEN COOKIES (3$\frac{1}{2}$ INCH)

1$\frac{1}{4}$ **cups packed brown sugar**

$\frac{1}{2}$ **cup shortening**

2 eggs

2$\frac{1}{2}$ **cups Original Bisquick mix**

1 cup old-fashioned or quick-cooking oats

1 cup candy-coated chocolate candies

$\frac{1}{2}$ **cup raisins**

$\frac{1}{2}$ **cup chopped nuts, if desired**

1 Heat oven to 375°F. In large bowl, beat brown sugar, shortening and eggs with electric mixer on medium speed, or mix with spoon until blended. Stir in remaining ingredients.

2 Onto ungreased cookie sheets, drop dough by $\frac{1}{4}$ cupfuls about 2 inches apart. With bottom of glass that has been greased and dipped into granulated sugar, flatten dough to about $\frac{1}{2}$-inch thickness.

3 Bake 12 to 16 minutes or until golden brown. Cool 3 minutes; carefully remove from cookie sheets to cooling racks.

1 COOKIE: Calories 270; Total Fat 11g (Saturated Fat 3.5g; Trans Fat 1.5g); Cholesterol 25mg; Sodium 260mg; Total Carbohydrate 39g (Dietary Fiber 1g); Protein 3g **Exchanges:** 1 Starch, 1$\frac{1}{2}$ Other Carbohydrate, 2 Fat **Carbohydrate Choices:** 2$\frac{1}{2}$

Quick Tip: Not a lot of free time? Make the dough a day earlier and refrigerate, then bake the cookies when you have a few spare minutes.

Peanut Butter–Pecan Chocolate Chip–Granola Cookies

PREP TIME: 1 HOUR 30 MINUTES   **START TO FINISH: 1 HOUR 30 MINUTES**
ABOUT 5 DOZEN COOKIES

1 cup butter, softened

1 cup creamy peanut butter

³/₄ cup granulated sugar

³/₄ cup packed brown sugar

1 teaspoon vanilla

2 eggs

2 cups Original Bisquick mix

1³/₄ cups granola cereal

1 cup milk chocolate chips

1 cup coarsely chopped pecans

1 Heat oven to 350°F. In large bowl, mix butter, peanut butter, sugars, vanilla and eggs with spoon. Stir in remaining ingredients. Onto ungreased cookie sheets, drop dough by rounded tablespoonfuls about 2 inches apart.

2 Bake 9 to 11 minutes or until edges are light golden brown (do not overbake). Cool 3 minutes; remove from cookie sheets to cooling racks.

1 COOKIE: Calories 140; Total Fat 8g (Saturated Fat 3.5g; Trans Fat 0g); Cholesterol 15mg; Sodium 95mg; Total Carbohydrate 13g (Dietary Fiber 0g); Protein 2g **Exchanges:** ¹/₂ Starch, ¹/₂ Other Carbohydrate, 1¹/₂ Fat **Carbohydrate Choices:** 1

BETTER WITH BISQUICK

Contest Winner:

**Amber Parsons •
Parkersburg, WV**

This delicious cookie won honorable mention in our Better with Bisquick Contest.

This is one cookie I don't mind my family eating in the morning before school or on the road. They are wholesome, with the granola cereal and peanut butter, and have enough sweetness to keep the kids happy.

Chocolate Chip Cookies

PREP TIME: 1 HOUR 20 MINUTES   START TO FINISH: 1 HOUR 20 MINUTES
ABOUT 4 ¹/₂ DOZEN COOKIES

¹/₂ cup butter or margarine, softened

1 cup packed brown sugar

2 teaspoons vanilla

1 egg

2 ³/₄ cups Original Bisquick mix

1 cup semisweet chocolate chips (6 oz)

¹/₂ cup chopped nuts, if desired

1 Heat oven to 375°F. In large bowl, mix butter, brown sugar, vanilla and egg. Stir in Bisquick mix, chocolate chips and nuts.

2 Onto ungreased cookie sheets, drop dough by rounded teaspoonfuls about 2 inches apart; flatten slightly.

3 Bake about 10 minutes or until golden brown. Remove from cookie sheets to cooling racks.

1 COOKIE: Calories 70; Total Fat 3.5g (Saturated Fat 2g; Trans Fat 0g); Cholesterol 10mg; Sodium 100mg; Total Carbohydrate 10g (Dietary Fiber 0g); Protein 0g **Exchanges:** ¹/₂ Other Carbohydrate, 1 Fat **Carbohydrate Choices:** ¹/₂

Quick Tip: Hard brown sugar? Place the sugar in a plastic bag with an apple wedge for a day or two to soften, then throw away the apple.

No-Roll Sugar Cookies

PREP TIME: 55 MINUTES   START TO FINISH: 55 MINUTES
ABOUT 4 DOZEN COOKIES

4 cups Original Bisquick mix

1½ cups powdered sugar

¾ cup butter or margarine, softened

1 teaspoon almond extract

2 eggs

1 cup colored granulated sugar

1 Heat oven to 400°F. In large bowl, stir all ingredients except granulated sugar until soft dough forms.

2 Shape dough into 1-inch balls; roll in colored granulated sugar to coat. On ungreased cookie sheets, place balls about 2 inches apart. Flatten balls slightly with bottom of glass.

3 Bake 5 to 6 minutes or until edges are light golden brown. Cool 1 minute; remove from cookie sheets to cooling racks. Store in airtight container.

1 COOKIE: Calories 100; Total Fat 4.5g (Saturated Fat 2.5g; Trans Fat 0g); Cholesterol 15mg; Sodium 150mg; Total Carbohydrate 14g (Dietary Fiber 0g); Protein 1g **Exchanges:** ½ Starch, ½ Other Carbohydrate, 1 Fat **Carbohydrate Choices:** 1

Quick Tip: Make cookies as directed—except drop dough by tablespoonfuls about 2 inches apart onto ungreased cookie sheet. Flatten with a sugared glass bottom. (Cookies will be less rounded.)

Lickety-Split Gingersnaps

PREP TIME: 45 MINUTES   START TO FINISH: 1 HOUR 5 MINUTES
ABOUT 4 DOZEN COOKIES

1 cup packed dark brown sugar

$^1/_3$ cup shortening

$^1/_4$ cup full-flavor (dark) molasses

1 egg

2$^1/_2$ cups Original Bisquick mix

1$^1/_2$ teaspoons ground allspice

1$^1/_2$ teaspoons ground ginger

2 tablespoons granulated sugar

1 Heat oven to 375°F. In large bowl, mix brown sugar, shortening, molasses and egg with spoon. Stir in Bisquick mix, allspice and ginger.

2 On work surface sprinkled with Bisquick mix, gently roll dough in Bisquick mix to coat. Divide dough into 4 parts. Shape each part into a roll, ¾ to 1 inch in diameter and about 12 inches long. On large ungreased cookie sheet, place rolls about 2 inches apart. Sprinkle granulated sugar down centers of rolls.

3 Bake 12 to 15 minutes or until set and slightly cracked. Cool on cookie sheet 5 minutes. Cut diagonally into about 1-inch strips. Carefully remove from cookie sheet to cooling rack.

1 COOKIE: Calories 70; Total Fat 2.5g (Saturated Fat 0.5g; Trans Fat 0g); Cholesterol 0mg; Sodium 80mg; Total Carbohydrate 10g (Dietary Fiber 0g); Protein 0g **Exchanges:** ½ Starch, ½ Fat **Carbohydrate Choices:** ½

Turtle Bars

PREP TIME: 10 MINUTES • START TO FINISH: 1 HOUR
36 BARS

1 cup Original Bisquick mix

1 cup quick-cooking oats

$^3/_4$ cup packed brown sugar

$^1/_4$ cup butter or margarine, melted

1 jar (12.25 oz) caramel topping

1$^1/_2$ cups pecan halves

1 cup swirled semisweet and white chocolate chips (6 oz)

1 Heat oven to 350°F. Line 13×9-inch pan with foil; spray with cooking spray. In large bowl, stir Bisquick mix, oats, brown sugar and butter until well blended. Press in bottom of pan.

2 Bake 15 to 18 minutes or until golden brown.

3 Remove pan from oven. Spread caramel topping over crust; sprinkle with pecan halves and chocolate chips. Bake 20 to 30 minutes longer or until caramel is bubbly. For bars, cut into 6 rows by 6 rows.

1 BAR: Calories 130; Total Fat 6g (Saturated Fat 2g; Trans Fat 0g); Cholesterol 0mg; Sodium 90mg; Total Carbohydrate 18g (Dietary Fiber 1g); Protein 1g **Exchanges:** 1 Other Carbohydrate, 1$^1/_2$ Fat **Carbohydrate Choices:** 1

Quick Tip: Lining the pan with foil and spraying the foil makes removing the bars easier and cleanup a breeze. Try this method with all of your bars!

Triple-Chocolate Bars

PREP TIME: 15 MINUTES   START TO FINISH: 2 HOURS 50 MINUTES
48 BARS

1 bag (12 oz) semisweet chocolate chips (2 cups)

2 packages (3 oz each) cream cheese

²⁄₃ cup evaporated milk

2 cups Original Bisquick mix

³⁄₄ cup sugar

¹⁄₂ cup unsweetened baking cocoa

³⁄₄ cup butter or margarine, softened

1 cup white vanilla baking chips

1 cup semisweet chocolate chips (6 oz)

1 Heat oven to 375°F. In 2-quart saucepan, heat 2 cups chocolate chips, the cream cheese and evaporated milk over low heat, stirring constantly, until chips are melted and mixture is smooth. Cool while making crust.

2 In medium bowl, mix Bisquick mix, sugar and cocoa. Using pastry blender (or pulling 2 table knives through ingredients in opposite directions), cut in butter until mixture looks like coarse crumbs.

3 Press half of Bisquick mixture (2 cups) in bottom of ungreased 13×9-inch pan. Sprinkle with vanilla baking chips. Spoon chocolate mixture over Bisquick mixture and chips; spread evenly. Sprinkle with remaining Bisquick mixture and 1 cup chocolate chips. Press lightly with fork.

4 Bake 30 to 35 minutes until center is set. Cool completely, about 1 hour. Refrigerate about 1 hour or until chilled. For bars, cut into 8 rows by 6 rows. Store covered in refrigerator.

1 BAR: Calories 160; Total Fat 10g (Saturated Fat 5g; Trans Fat 0g); Cholesterol 15mg; Sodium 110mg; Total Carbohydrate 16g (Dietary Fiber 0g); Protein 2g **Exchanges:** 1 Other Carbohydrate, 2 Fat **Carbohydrate Choices:** 1

Quick Tip: Surprise a chocolate lover with these decadent bars baked in a disposable pan. For a special touch, add ¹⁄₂ cup chopped walnuts or pecans with the white vanilla baking chips for an extra indulgence.

Glazed Lemon Bars

PREP TIME: 15 MINUTES   START TO FINISH: 1 HOUR 50 MINUTES
24 BARS

BASE

1 cup Bisquick Heart Smart mix

2 tablespoons powdered sugar

2 tablespoons cold butter or margarine

FILLING

¾ cup granulated sugar

½ cup fat-free egg product, 4 egg whites or 2 eggs

1 tablespoon Bisquick Heart Smart mix

2 teaspoons grated lemon peel

2 tablespoons lemon juice

GLAZE

¾ cup powdered sugar

1 tablespoon plus 1½ teaspoons lemon juice

Lemon peel

1 Heat oven to 350°F. In small bowl, mix 1 cup Bisquick mix and the powdered sugar. Using pastry blender or fork, cut in butter until mixture looks like fine crumbs. In ungreased 8-inch square pan, press mixture in bottom and ½ inch up sides.

2 Bake about 10 minutes or until light brown. Meanwhile, in small bowl, mix filling ingredients.

3 Pour filling over partially baked base. Bake about 25 minutes longer or until set and golden brown. Meanwhile, in small bowl, stir glaze ingredients until smooth.

4 While bars are warm, loosen edges from sides of pan. Spread glaze over bars. Cool completely, about 1 hour. For bars, cut into 6 rows by 4 rows. Garnish with lemon peel.

1 BAR: Calories 80; Total Fat 1.5g (Saturated Fat 0.5g; Trans Fat 0g); Cholesterol 0mg; Sodium 65mg; Total Carbohydrate 17g (Dietary Fiber 0g); Protein 1g **Exchanges:** 1 Other Carbohydrate, ½ Fat **Carbohydrate Choices:** 1

Quick Tip: One fresh lemon will give you 2 to 3 tablespoons of juice. To get the most juice out of a lemon, it should be at room temperature. To quickly warm whole lemons, put them in the microwave on High for about 20 seconds or so.

Metric Conversion Guide

VOLUME

U.S. Units	Canadian Metric	Australian Metric
1/4 teaspoon	1 mL	1 ml
1/2 teaspoon	2 mL	2 ml
1 teaspoon	5 mL	5 ml
1 tablespoon	15 mL	20 ml
1/4 cup	50 mL	60 ml
1/3 cup	75 mL	80 ml
1/2 cup	125 mL	125 ml
2/3 cup	150 mL	170 ml
3/4 cup	175 mL	190 ml
1 cup	250 mL	250 ml
1 quart	1 liter	1 liter
1 1/2 quarts	1.5 liters	1.5 liters
2 quarts	2 liters	2 liters
2 1/2 quarts	2.5 liters	2.5 liters
3 quarts	3 liters	3 liters
4 quarts	4 liters	4 liters

WEIGHT

U.S. Units	Canadian Metric	Australian Metric
1 ounce	30 grams	30 grams
2 ounces	55 grams	60 grams
3 ounces	85 grams	90 grams
4 ounces (1/4 pound)	115 grams	125 grams
8 ounces (1/2 pound)	225 grams	225 grams
16 ounces (1 pound)	455 grams	500 grams
1 pound	455 grams	1/2 kilogram

MEASUREMENTS

Inches	Centimeters
1	2.5
2	5.0
3	7.5
4	10.0
5	12.5
6	15.0
7	17.5
8	20.5
9	23.0
10	25.5
11	28.0
12	30.5
13	33.0

TEMPERATURES

Fahrenheit	Celsius
32°	0°
212°	100°
250°	120°
275°	140°
300°	150°
325°	160°
350°	180°
375°	190°
400°	200°
425°	220°
450°	230°
475°	240°
500°	260°

NOTE: The recipes in this cookbook have not been developed or tested using metric measures. When converting recipes to metric, some variations in quality may be noted.

Index

Page numbers in *italics* indicate illustrations

**Recommended intake for a
daily diet of 2,000 calories
as set by the Food and Drug
Administration**

Total Fat	Less than 65g
Saturated Fat	Less than 20g
Cholesterol	Less than 300mg
Sodium	Less than 2,400mg
Total Carbohydrate	300g
Dietary Fiber	25g

Complete your cookbook library with these *Betty Crocker* titles

Betty Crocker 300 Calorie Cookbook

Betty Crocker Baking for Today

Betty Crocker Basics

Betty Crocker's Best Bread Machine Cookbook

Betty Crocker's Best Chicken Cookbook

Betty Crocker's Best Christmas Cookbook

Betty Crocker's Best of Baking

Betty Crocker's Best of Healthy and Hearty Cooking

Betty Crocker's Best-Loved Recipes

Betty Crocker Big Book of Cupcakes

Betty Crocker Big Book of Slow Cooker, Casseroles & More

Betty Crocker's Bisquick® Cookbook

Betty Crocker Bisquick® II Cookbook

Betty Crocker Bisquick® Impossibly Easy Pies

Betty Crocker Bisquick® to the Rescue

Betty Crocker Celebrate!

Betty Crocker Christmas

Betty Crocker's Complete Thanksgiving Cookbook

Betty Crocker's Cook Book for Boys and Girls

Betty Crocker's Cook It Quick

Betty Crocker Cookbook, 10th Edition— *The* **BIG RED** *Cookbook*®

Betty Crocker Cookbook, Bridal Edition

Betty Crocker's Cookie Book

Betty Crocker's Cooking Basics

Betty Crocker's Cooking for Two

Betty Crocker's Cooky Book, Facsimile Edition

Betty Crocker Country Cooking

Betty Crocker Decorating Cakes and Cupcakes

Betty Crocker's Diabetes Cookbook

Betty Crocker Dinner Made Easy with Rotisserie Chicken

Betty Crocker Easy Everyday Vegetarian

Betty Crocker Easy Family Dinners

Betty Crocker's Easy Slow Cooker Dinners

Betty Crocker's Eat and Lose Weight

Betty Crocker's Entertaining Basics

Betty Crocker's Flavors of Home

Betty Crocker 4-Ingredient Dinners

Betty Crocker Grilling Made Easy

Betty Crocker Healthy Heart Cookbook

Betty Crocker's Healthy New Choices

Betty Crocker's Indian Home Cooking

Betty Crocker's Italian Cooking

Betty Crocker's Kids Cook!

Betty Crocker's Kitchen Library

Betty Crocker's Living with Cancer Cookbook

Betty Crocker Low-Carb Lifestyle Cookbook

Betty Crocker's Low-Fat, Low-Cholesterol Cooking Today

Betty Crocker Money Saving Meals

Betty Crocker More Slow Cooker Recipes

Betty Crocker's New Cake Decorating

Betty Crocker's New Chinese Cookbook

Betty Crocker One-Dish Meals

Betty Crocker's A Passion for Pasta

Betty Crocker's Picture Cook Book, Facsimile Edition

Betty Crocker's Quick & Easy Cookbook

Betty Crocker's Slow Cooker Cookbook

Betty Crocker's Ultimate Cake Mix Cookbook

Betty Crocker's Vegetarian Cooking

Betty Crocker Why It Works